THE WEALTH OF RELIGIONS

The Wealth
of Religions

The Political
Economy of Believing
and Belonging

Rachel M. McCleary and Robert J. Barro

PRINCETON UNIVERSITY PRESS

PRINCETON AND OXFORD

Published by Princeton University Press
41 William Street, Princeton, New Jersey 08540
6 Oxford Street, Woodstock, Oxfordshire OX20 1TR

press.princeton.edu

Library of Congress Control Number: 2019930185
ISBN 978-0-691-17895-0

British Library Cataloging-in-Publication Data is available

Editorial: Joe Jackson and Jacqueline Delaney
Production Editorial: Jenny Wolkowicki
Jacket design: Faceout Studio, Lindy Martin
Production: Erin Suydam
Publicity: James Schneider and Caroline Priday
Copyeditor: Joseph Dahm

Jacket credit: Shutterstock

This book has been composed in Modern

Printed on acid-free paper. ∞

Printed in the United States of America

10 9 8 7 6 5 4 3 2 1

CONTENTS

With Robert as an economist and Rachel as a moral philosopher, we bring a diversity of tools and perspectives to study the nature of human agency and the beliefs on which humans choose to act. Whereas sociologists and economists before us applied economic principles and ideas to religion treating it as a social construct, we took a different tact. We took as our starting point Max Weber's (1864–1920) argument that religious beliefs motivate people to be productive, through inculcated values such as diligence, integrity, and thrift. Our analysis stresses the role of religious beliefs, especially those related to an afterlife (heaven, hell), in underpinning individual traits. In our interpretation, participation in formal religious activities, religious education, and time spent on personal prayer matter mainly by affecting religious beliefs and character traits. Effectively, there is a religion production function in which time and other resources are inputs and in which beliefs and values are the principal outputs. These individual traits matter for productivity and, thereby, for economic growth.

The chapters in this volume are based on articles published over the course of sixteen years of our joint work. We begin the book by presenting our basic conceptual framework. We discuss the connection between religion and economic behavior by looking at a two-way causation: the effect of economic growth on religion and vice versa. We intellectually ground our framework in Adam Smith's approach to competition in his *Wealth of Nations* and Max Weber's views on beliefs and character traits in his *Protestant Ethic and the Spirit of Capitalism*. We introduce modern analyses by sociologists and economists. From this conceptual framework, we move to other topics that extend our ideas as well as those of other scholars working in this area.

Since 2001, we have hosted a seminar series at Harvard on the political economy of religion. The seminar was made possible by funding from the John Templeton Foundation, the Lynde and Harry Bradley Foundation, Harvard's Paul M. Warburg Fund, and the Provost's Office of Harvard University. Hundreds of scholars and students have participated and presented their work in the seminar series and at two conferences we hosted with the Harvard Divinity School. Gratitude is due to all the seminar participants for sharing ideas and engaging in lively discussions that furthered our understanding but, more significantly, for making significant contributions to the economics and sociology of religion.

We are particularly indebted to our Harvard colleagues, William Hutchison (deceased), David Hall, Paul Peterson, Leonard van der Kuijp, Asim Khwaja, Filipe Campante, David Yanagizawa-Drott, Edward Glaeser, and Nathan Nunn, for their intellectual engagement, their support, and their own contributions. Robert Ekelund, Robert Hébert, and Robert Tollison (deceased) early on actively encouraged us to pursue this work.

We have benefited from discussions with numerous colleagues and students, for which we express our gratitude. We owe a special debt of thanks to the following individuals for interacting with us over several years: Laurence Iannaccone, Sascha Becker, Timur Kuran, Murat Iyigun, Eli Berman, Evelyn Lehrer, Mark Chaves, Roger Finke, Grace Davie, Charles Keyes, Jared Rubin, Sriya Iyer, Jose Ursúa, Ran Abramitzky, Paul Froese, Eric Chaney, Jonathan Fox, Daniel Chen, Davide Cantone, Ricardo Perez-Truglia, Brian Wheaton, Jason Hwang, and Alexander McQuoid.

A special note of thanks to Joe Jackson, Senior Editor at Princeton University Press, whom we first met when he was at Oxford University Press. We are pleased to be working with Joe. Two unidentified reviewers read the manuscript (even though we think we know who they are). We welcomed their comments and suggestions with the anticipation of making it a better book.

THE WEALTH OF RELIGIONS

Religion

IT'S A MARKET

Robert and I were sitting in a doctor's waiting room. An elderly man and his son came in and sat down in the chairs opposite us. After a few moments, the man addressed Robert, "You must be a man of the cloth." Surprised at the comment, Robert asked, "Why do you say that?" The man responded, "You are dressed in black and the tips of your shoes are worn from kneeling."

Just as the elderly man in the doctor's waiting room mistakenly identified Robert as a priest, people sometimes react to our seminars and classes on religion and economy as though we were religious professionals or at least committed adherents. Almost without fail, questions arise about our personal religious beliefs. One answer that works well is to draw an analogy with a colleague who studied the economics of crime. When he gave a seminar on this topic, no one asked him whether he was a criminal. So why is the political economy of religion something different?

There are good reasons why a social-science academic inquiry into religion differs from the study of other topics. Religion is personal. People are not being narrow or unreasonable when they respond to our research by asking about our personal religious beliefs.

Individual religiosity is a potent force in people's daily lives. It is natural that one would like to understand how our own religious tendencies and beliefs inform the questions we seek to answer; how we understand religious beliefs, rituals, and organizations; and how we interpret our work in furthering human understanding of religious phenomena. People may think that, if a researcher is an atheist, she might have difficulty in finding that religiosity tends to improve people's lives. And, conversely, if someone is a committed adherent, he might find it hard to conclude that religion has adverse effects.

Others who ask us about our religious background and beliefs view religion as a cultural fabrication, an archaic vestige of primitive societies akin to superstitions and new age spiritualism. On this view, religion is irrational. These individuals view being religious as compromising the ability of a researcher to carry out objective analyses of the interplay between religion and political economy. If religion is important in a researcher's own life, she might not easily reach the conclusion that religiosity has beneficial and harmful effects on individual behavior and institutional outcomes.

Many atheists, such as the physicist Carl Sagan and philosopher Tim Crane, maintain a respectful understanding of religion. For example, Sagan ([1985] 2006, pp. 148–168), in his Gifford Lectures, concluded that the existence of God can be neither proved nor disproved; only specific conceptualizations can be evaluated. This conclusion had been reached earlier by many scholars, including Sigmund Freud. And, like Freud, Sagan thought that some aspects of religion, particularly prayer, can have a positive effect on people, even those who do not believe in God. The importance of prayer for nonbelievers was borne out by a recent survey in Britain; a quarter of atheists and agnostics pray even though they do not believe in God and do not believe that a deity hears their prayers (Alex Green 2018).

As an atheist, Crane (2017) views religion through a postmodern, scientific lens. Religion, like scientific endeavor, attempts to impose order on chaos, to explain the natural world with transcendental "truths" and beliefs. Crane posits that the difference between science and religion is that although both seek to explain our universe, religion comfortably accommodates the unintelligible in our world whereas science strives to continually explain it.

As investigators, we are not just objective observers and recorders of experience but also active participants. According to the philosopher Stephen Toulmin (1982, pp. 209–210), "Our place is within the same world that we are studying, and whatever scientific understanding we achieve must be a kind of understanding that is available to participants within the process of nature, i.e., from inside." Thus, as academic investigators, we bring our own perspectives to the context, the circumstances we are studying. Yet, it is also our responsibility as researchers to be cognizant of the implicit conceptions we function with and how to question them in light of empirical findings from our own research and that of other scholars.

Another philosopher, Thomas Nagel (1986), who sought a balance between subjective and objective knowing, argues for a more objective perspective. "The truth is sometimes best understood from a detached standpoint," he claims. Objectivity makes possible the intellectual creation of theories, the advancement of knowledge, and ultimately the attainment of truth. Nagel proposes that this perspective is acquired through a gradual process of detachment but should never be total detachment. Such perspective is false—objective blindness—and ends in the Cartesian fallacy: "I think, therefore I am." The "exploration and reorganization of the insides of our own minds" becomes the research topic and not the hypothesis we set out to investigate. Conducting research on religion is sensitive because it is personal. But we agree with Nagel that we need to be detached observers, impartial to the outcomes of our investigations.

An additional factor is that colleges and universities around the world, not just in the United States, bifurcate the sciences from the humanities. Methods of inquiry in the physical and social sciences, as well as topics considered legitimate for "scientific inquiry," are secular in many dimensions. As Nagel (1986, p. 9) expresses it, "Scientism is a form of idealism ... at its most myopic it assumes that everything there is must be understandable by the employment of scientific theories." Questions about religion have been viewed, until recently, with intellectual skepticism as being outside the realm of empirical and "scientific" investigation.

We view our approach as a corrective measure for the study of religion in higher education. A social-science approach to religion is valid in that it seeks to answer questions about how religions evolve, compete, make us richer or poorer, and influence the daily lives of people around the world. The economics of religion does not concern itself, per se, with theology, doctrine, and the content of religious beliefs. Rather, we are interested in the economic costs and benefits to holding certain religious beliefs and the influence of those beliefs on behavior. We agree with Charles L. Glenn's (2017, p. 77) position that secularists within and outside academia seeking to "drive other worldviews from the public square, or from educational institutions, or from the practices of voluntary associations, is nothing less than tyranny." We want religion to be part of the discussion in the social sciences, even in a highly secular institution such as Harvard University.

As academic investigators, what is our standpoint? From what perspective do we examine and interact with the religions we are studying? We are pretty sure that we are carrying out objective research that seeks to understand how religion influences and is influenced by economic, political, and social forces. By constantly reflecting upon our assumptions, methodology, and findings, we can reach some understanding. That is, we are participating in a "search for truth," not an attempt to advocate or denigrate religion. But readers will have to judge how successful we are in this effort. And we are surely not going to say anything at this point about our personal religious beliefs!

The Economics of Religion—Beliefs Are Mostly What Matter

When we think about religion, we consider the institutions and individuals who participate. To be religious does not require membership in an institution. However, the survival of a religious institution depends on the participation of its adherents. Competition for followers among religious organizations is regulated by the marketplace of religion. Our approach to this marketplace focuses on religious beliefs, such as in salvation, damnation, an afterlife, and supernatural beings such as a god or gods, angels, and demons. We particularly want to analyze the implications of holding those beliefs for human behavior. Religious beliefs—not per se participation in organized religion and personal prayer—are important guiding mechanisms for economic behavior.

Religious beliefs are powerful incentives to behave according to the moral teachings of one's religion. If people believe that through their own efforts they can improve their chances of attaining salvation, then it makes sense that they will inculcate the moral values taught by their religion and act accordingly. Moral values, such as dedication to work, thrift, honesty, and trustworthiness, constrain a person's behavior with the aim of improving her chances of a better afterlife (attaining heaven as opposed to hell). The anticipated afterlife benefits motivate believers to behave in prescribed moral ways and to invest their time in religious activities.

We take seriously sociologist Max Weber's ([1904–1905] 1930) argument in his famous book, *The Protestant Ethic and the Spirit of Capitalism*, that religious beliefs foster traits, such as work ethic, honesty, and thrift, that contribute to economic growth. We also view distributive economic activities—tithing to religious institutions, donating to secular charities, and funding the establishment of religious schools—as possibly enhancing economic activity. In short, religion can promote economic growth through the religious beliefs and practices imparted to its adherents.

Economists Corry Azzi and Ronald Ehrenberg (1975) found by incorporating religious activity into household choices that the economic value of time (the real wage rate for people working in the formal labor market) affects the time that an individual allocates to religious activities. Their analysis predicted a U-shaped pattern of religious participation over the life cycle. In youth, the economic value of time is low, and high investment in religious activities makes sense. When a person enters the workforce, time becomes highly valued and investment in religion declines. When a person reaches retirement age, the value of time decreases and participation in religion again becomes high.

This life-cycle model of religious participation accords with a pattern whereby a person sometimes reduces time spent on formal religion—such as in middle age—without losing faith. That is, a person can continue to believe strongly while simultaneously spending less time on formal religion. The argument is that religious beliefs motivate people to be diligent at their work, save to support their family, and be trustworthy in relations with colleagues and friends *even though* they may not participate in religious activities as much as they did in the past.

According to economist George Stigler (1982, pp. 22–23), religious activities are similar to commercial transactions in that they are voluntary and repetitive. Because they are voluntary, they must make each rational person at least as well off as before the transaction. Because they are repetitive, religious activities promote honesty, transparency, and trust and create an environment in which participants resist the temptation to cheat and lie. As with other economic agents, Stigler viewed religious believers as utility-maximizers, who weigh the costs and benefits of participation in a religion.

In the mid-1980s, an innovative approach to the study of religion took off, based on ideas in Adam Smith's *Wealth of Nations* (1791) and *Theory of Moral Sentiments* (1797). This new research was motivated in part by the rise in the 1950s and 1960s of US utopian religious communities that attracted thousands of people, young, old, and families with children. Some of these movements were unorthodox Christian sects led by charismatic leaders, such as Jim Jones with his Peoples Temple (ultimately responsible for the mass suicide and murder in Guyana in 1978) and the Reverend Sun Myung Moon with his Unification Church. Others were Hindu ashrams formed around a guru or swami, such as Maharishi Mahesh Yogi, who became the spiritual guide of the Beatles and started the Students International Meditation Society. The heterodox nature of these cults in terms of beliefs, practices, and organization raised

questions about the voluntary nature of conversions to these movements. Why would someone follow an Indian guru or self-appointed
Christian apostle whose religion required significant sacrifice and
stigmatic behavior? The characterization of conversion to a cult as
a form of involuntary "indoctrination," "brainwashing," "mental pro-
gramming," and "mind control" became a controversial and popular topic.[1]

Economist Laurence Iannaccone saw the attractiveness of the
new religious movements differently. Iannaccone (1992) demonstrated that the psychological characteristics of converts to radical
sects and cults were no different from those of the general Christian population, who belonged to Protestant denominations or the
Catholic Church. Applying a rational-choice approach to new religious movements, Iannaccone argued that people voluntarily chose
to participate in a religion based on maximizing their objectives
through a cost-benefit analysis. Basic economic principles, summa-
rized by Gary Becker (1976, p. 5) as "maximizing behavior, market
equilibrium, and stable preferences," were fruitfully applied by
Iannaccone (1988) in a formal model to understand individuals'
choices of religion.

In religion, maximizing behavior translates into finding a group
or church (temple, mosque, or synagogue) that satisfies one's religious needs. We can view religious groups as providing services
that people consume. For example, rituals, doctrines, and beliefs
are types of religious products that a person chooses. We think of
these religious goods as falling on a continuum in terms of strictness at one end and laxness at the other.[2] The stricter the goods of
a religious group, the higher the degree of distinctiveness, separation, and possibly antagonism between the religious group and its
societal context. The higher the tension between a religious group
and its surroundings, the costlier it is to belong to that group. Those
religious groups with low tension with the sociocultural environment tend to be more accommodating of the secular world.

Using a version of the club model developed by James Buchanan
(1965), Iannaccone demonstrated that the strict requirements of a
cult kept out less enthusiastic people (free riders), while maintaining

a high-quality religious experience for those who retained membership and highly valued the organization. Requiring a strong commitment through sacrifice and stigmatic behavior can enrich the religious experience of members.

Iannaccone's club model explains why utility-maximizing individuals are motivated to join a radical sect with a reward structure deviating from the societal norm. The German sociologist Max Weber, during his tour of the United States in 1904, noted that a compelling motive to join a Christian sect with "ruthlessly rigorous control over the conduct of their members" was to gain a highly religious experience, including salvation.[3] Affiliating with a sect signaled that a convert was willing to be equally as religious as the other members of the sect. Acceptance by one's fellow believers was more important than being accepted by outsiders, including family and friends.

The club model has also been used to explain why people join violent religious groups, such as Hamas, ISIS, and the Taliban, as well as commercial communal groups, such as the kibbutzim in Israel.[4] In the cases of radical Islamic groups, potential fighters compare different fighting groups by weighing the benefits and costs. Benefits for fighters include a salary and material goods, but also insurance such as medical care, postmortem arrangements for deceased fighters, and support for their families. Since there are no official insurance guarantees (and little power to enforce any in a war-torn country), fighters have to rely on a group's reputation (Mironova 2017).

From the Islamic rebel group's perspective, only the most trustworthy and loyal prospective fighters are worth attracting as members. To identify these individuals and to minimize defections, radical Islamic groups make membership costly by requiring adherence to a strict religious code that has no direct bearing on the prospective member's fighting abilities. Members of Islamist rebel groups, for example, are required to wear traditional clothes, pray five times a day, and refrain from consumption of tobacco and alcohol. These religious rules stress group homogeneity and loyalty critical to survival in an armed rebellion. The religious rules also stress conduct signaling true belief in Islam, a trait supporting engagement in ideological warfare. To be the most effective fighting group, a balance is struck between using ideology as a screening mechanism and preventing it from affecting groups' military and political strategies.

Until the 1990s, empirical research on political economy typically neglected the influence of religion. However, the work by Azzi and Ehrenberg (1975) and Iannaccone (1988) opened up the application of economic principles to various aspects of religion, and recent research on political economy has often included dimensions of religion. One important topic is how religiosity responds to economic development and to government regulation, subsidy, and suppression. Other questions concern why some countries establish and maintain official state religions and how state subsidies and regulations influence religious activities. Also important is how religious beliefs and practices affect productivity, economic growth, and the maintenance of political institutions such as democracy. Recent research, for example, considers how economic growth responds to different degrees of religious beliefs and participation in organized religion.

Our central approach is the application of economic and political principles to the study of religions across countries and over time. As an example, people face trade-offs when practicing a religion. The time spent on religious services could be used instead to engage with friends and family, participate in a sport or exercise, travel, watch television, read, or go to the shopping mall. However, participation in religious rituals and services also conveys benefits. Practitioners gain from the communal worship experience of singing, praying, reading the Bible, hearing a sermon, and interacting with people who share their faith and beliefs. People also benefit from the strengthening of religious beliefs that results from participation in formal religious services. This benefit is especially important when raising one's children in a formal religion. Each person implicitly weighs these costs and benefits when deciding how much to participate in religious activities.

A basic ingredient in the economics of religion is that people systematically and purposefully strive to achieve their objectives.

That is, *rational choice* applies to religion as much as to other individual and social decisions. To use economic terminology, we "purchase" religious goods in the sense of expending time and resources on religion. If a religion demands that you go to formal services every week or pray five times a day, donate 20 percent of your income, wear distinctive clothing, or follow a specific diet, you may decide it is too costly and opt to reduce your participation or choose a cheaper religion. As a believer, you are a consumer of religious goods and services; that is, you have a demand for religion.

There is also a supply of religion—some of it coming from organized religion in the form of formal religious services. We analyze the incentives of these organizations and, particularly, how they are influenced by government regulation of the religion market. The presence of an official or state religion is an important component of this regulation.

What Is in This Book?

The book is divided into two sections, which emphasize different applications of economics to the study of religion. In the first section, the chapters deal with the interplay between religion and economic growth.

Chapter 2 introduces the two-way interaction between religion and economic growth—economic outcomes influence religiousness and, in turn, religiousness affects economic outcomes. This chapter then examines the first causal direction—how do economic growth and government regulation of the religion market affect religious participation and beliefs?

One key idea is the *secularization* hypothesis, whereby increases in income, education, urbanization, and life expectancy are thought to diminish individual religiousness and the role of religion in governance. In extreme—and counterfactual—versions, growing education and scientific orientation are thought to sharply diminish the demand for religion. Another key concept is the religion-market model, which argues that government regulation including the establishment of a state religion can influence the extent of competition in the religion market (religious diversity) and thereby affect the quality of religion products and the extent of religious participation.

Secularization applied to some aspects of John Calvin's city of Geneva and its regulation of economic activity, especially the distinction doctrinally made between interest and usury. Interest was an economic necessity for commercial and financial transactions and was allowed by the authorities. The maximum interest rate, set at 5 percent, was regulated by the Genevan government and the Consistory, a corporate religious-moral committee of the government whose judgments were enforced by the city council (using public censure, excommunication, incarceration, and banishment). Charging interest at a rate above 5 percent was viewed as usury, in the sense of constituting "excessive" interest. Usury in this form was scripturally banned and triggered a punishment set by the Consistory.

During Calvin's lifetime, the ceiling interest rate was raised from 5 to 6.7 percent, and after his death in 1564, the Genevan government increased the rate further to 10 percent (Robert Kingdon 1959, pp. 37–38). Nicolas Colladon, a friend of Calvin's and secretary of the Company of Pastors, publicly denounced the interest rate hike from his pulpit. The Company of Pastors, rather than supporting Colladon's theological position, expelled him from the Company, setting the stage for Colladon's exile from Geneva. The wholesale clerical abandonment of Calvin's theological stance on interest versus usury and the siding with the Genevan government's decree of raising the legal interest rate began the secularization of economic activity in Geneva.

Chapter 3 examines the other causal direction—how does religiousness affect economic and political outcomes? In this chapter, we cover themes and arguments laid out by Max Weber in his *Protestant Ethic and the Spirit of Capitalism* ([1904–1905] 1930). Weber looked for "the influence of certain religious ideas on the development of the economic spirit, or the *ethos* of an economic system" (p. 27).

Using quantitative analysis of modern data, we find that economic growth responds positively to higher religious beliefs—notably those related to hell and heaven—when measured relative to religious participation (gauged particularly by attendance at formal religious services). We think that the beliefs matter (positively) mostly by promoting traits such as work effort and thrift, as stressed by Weber. We think that participation matters (negatively) mostly because it represents consumption of resources and, also, proxies for negative economic and legal regulation. Another channel of effects is that Protestantism's stress on individual reading of the Bible led to higher literacy and, thereby, promoted economic development.

In Chapter 4 we focus on Islam, especially its legal and economic regulations. Geographic regions under Muslim control excelled at scientific discovery through the eleventh century and at military prowess through the sixteenth century. However, Muslim countries declined sharply economically relative to Christian countries since the Industrial Revolution beginning in the seventeenth century. As argued by Timur Kuran (2004), Muslim countries were held back by restrictions on corporate legal form, inheritance, credit and insurance markets, and contract enforcement. These legal institutions and markets became particularly important with the expanded scale of business organizations due to the Industrial Revolution, hence the relative economic decline of Muslim societies starting in the seventeenth century.

The second section of the book has three chapters that emphasize the connection between religion and political economy. Chapter 5 focuses on state religion, which played a role in our analysis of religiousness. We try to explain why some countries have state religions and others do not. State religions—which we gauge more by practice than by legal provisions—tend to arise when most people in a country belong to a single religion. This pattern holds independently of the type of religion, with a small additional positive effect when the main religion is Islam. Higher economic development has little impact on the probability of having a state religion, but population has an inverted-U effect—countries with high population (such as India) and with low population are unlikely to have an official religion. Communist countries almost never have a state religion. There is also a remarkable durability of state religion.

Choices made centuries ago, such as the split between Catholicism and Protestantism with the Reformation in England and Sweden in the 1500s and with the Schism between the Eastern and Western Christian Churches in Constantinople in 1054, still matter a lot for the shape of today's religious institutions.

In Chapter 6, we view organized religious groups, including cults, as Buchanan-Iannaccone clubs in which members sometimes endure high costs of belonging in order to screen out free riders who do not contribute to the group's mission and social cohesiveness. We apply this framework to terrorist organizations and argue that it helps to explain aspects of religious-based violence, such as in Palestinian territory.

The tendency of scholars has been to apply the economics of religion approach to monotheistic religions. Examples are the rise of Protestantism in Europe (Robert Ekelund et al. 1996) and the connection of wars between Catholics and Protestants in Europe to the military status of the Ottoman Empire (Murat Iyigun 2008). Economist Sriya Iyer (2018) has applied ideas from the economics of religion to assess the role of Hindu and Muslim nonprofit organizations in India.

Also in Chapter 6, we incorporate our findings on state religion from Chapter 5 into the club framework to explain the rise of Buddhism to the status of a state religion in Tibet from the fifteenth century through the seventeenth. In an unregulated religion market such as the Tibet region in the twelfth century, a natural monopoly may arise. A critical element for sustaining monopoly is the presence of large fixed costs, such as those applicable to the creation and dissemination of a set of religious beliefs (for example, the construction of monasteries, patronage for the performance of merit-making rituals, the commissioning of editions of sacred texts, and the authoring of biographies). Relative to these fixed costs, the costs of membership and participation in alternative religions are small. Therefore, if people view these alternatives as close substitutes, a single type of religion might prevail in equilibrium. In the case of Tibet, this principal type turned out to be Mahayana Buddhism.

In Chapter 7 we continue the competition theme by looking at the Catholic Church's practice of saint making as a mechanism for countering the presence of Protestantism, especially evangelicals. Saint making works by reigniting religious fervor in traditionally Catholic regions. We also view saint making as a way to counter the rising tendency of Catholics to leave religion entirely. We look favorably on the Catholic Church's increased naming of blessed persons overall and in places, such as in Latin America, that were apart from the traditional emphasis on Italy and the rest of Europe. This globalization of saints applies also to popes, with the last three choices all coming from countries other than Italy. The increased naming of popular ex-popes as blessed persons is another way that the Catholic Church is attempting to enhance its popularity among its congregants.

Throughout the chapters, we employ economic concepts and principles. However, our approach is interdisciplinary, combining economic principles with sociology, anthropology, history, geography, theology, and philosophy. We believe that this type of interdisciplinary research will be critical to further advances in this field.

Hopefully, this book will persuade readers that an economic and social-science perspective is useful for understanding the interactions between religion and society. We are excited about how much we have learned about how religion matters, and we hope that readers will share in this excitement.

2

What Determines Religiousness?

Religion offers unique beliefs about the transcendent, be it a deity (monotheism) or deities (polytheism). We view a person as religious if he or she believes in a transcendent being or beings with supernatural powers that can intervene in human affairs. With this definition, religion is more than a community of believers who share a tradition of narratives, customs, norms, and rituals. It is also more than a network of social interactions and collective support. Being religious means having beliefs about human interaction with the transcendent.

Religiousness has a two-way interaction with political economy.[1] First, with religion viewed as a *dependent* variable, a central question is how economic development and political institutions affect religious participation and beliefs. One aspect of this interaction involves the influences on religiousness from growing income, education, urbanization, and life expectancy. Another dimension concerns effects on religiousness from the government's regulating religious activity, possibly including the establishment of a state religion. In this chapter, we study the first direction of causation— what determines religiousness in a country?

Second, in Chapter 3, we examine the effects of religion on economic, social, and political behavior. With religion as an *independent* variable, a key issue is how religiosity affects individual traits—such as work ethic, honesty, and thrift—and thereby influences economic performance. We interpret character traits such as industry, discipline, honesty, and law abidance as forms of human capital, in a way analogous to education and training. Another channel involves religion's effects on literacy and education more broadly and, thereby, on economic productivity. In addition, economic outcomes can change because of religion-inspired laws and regulations. These restrictions may impact financial markets, corporate structure, and inheritance and also affect gender roles, fertility, work hours, and store openings (such as blue laws that curtail business on Sundays).

Demand for Religion and the Secularization Hypothesis

In this chapter, we explore the first direction of causation: how the economy and the regulatory system influence religion in a society. When thinking of religion as a dependent variable, we can break down our analysis into demand-side and supply-side approaches, though economists instinctively look jointly at demand and supply. An influential demand-side analysis is the *secularization hypothesis*. In this framework, economic development reduces individual participation in formal religious activities, sometimes to the extent of disaffiliating with organized religion as well as diminishing the influence of organized religion on political choices and governance. Economic development also decreases religious beliefs and engagement in personal prayer. However, these interactions do not necessarily imply that secularization leads to atheism; in other words, declining religiosity is not the same as rejecting religion.

The secularization hypothesis goes back at least to the sermon on "The Use of Money" by the founder of Methodism, John Wesley, who observed (1978, pp. 258–261) that, as his congregants became richer, they became less devout. A fuller version of this hypothesis is in the German sociologist Max Weber's ([1904–1905] 1930) classic work, *The Protestant Ethic and the Spirit of Capitalism*, and Weber's ideas were extended by the sociologists Peter Berger (1967) and Bryan Wilson (1966).

According to Weber, economic development reduces the influence of organized religion on political decision making and, more generally, on economic, social, and legal processes. The secularization process also shows up in individuals becoming less religious, as measured by attendance at formal religious services and, most importantly for Weber, in the extent of religious beliefs.

For Weber, secularization was a reaction to the central role of religion during the Industrial Revolution in Europe during the 1700s and early 1800s. Weber thought that Protestantism was important in the early phases of the Industrial Revolution—for example, in Germany and Britain—because it provided moral discipline and a psychological compulsion to work hard (his thesis of the Protestant ethic). Technological advances such as the assembly line and automated machinery required a workforce that was willing to perform monotonous, repetitive jobs. However, Weber (p. 72) thought that, by the late nineteenth century, morality and work ethic had separated from otherworldly compensators such as salvation and damnation. Modern capitalism had created an internal foundation for the pursuit of self-interest and a "devotion to the calling of making money." Most importantly, this foundation no longer depended on religion. Thus, Weber declared that "modern capitalism has become dominant and has become emancipated from its old supports."

In any event, Weber believed that the Industrial Revolution—and, more broadly, economic success—would lead to a decline in individual religious participation and beliefs. The beliefs may refer to God, an afterlife, heaven, hell, and so forth, or may refer just to tendencies of people to characterize themselves as spiritual rather than affiliating with a particular religion, denomination, or sect. Empirical evidence that we discuss later bears out the hypothesis that, as a country becomes richer, religious participation and beliefs tend to fall.

Extreme views on secularization were presented by the Scottish philosopher David Hume ([1757] 1993), who viewed religious beliefs as mainly reflections of fear and ignorance. The founder of psychoanalysis Sigmund Freud argued that religion is an illusion, based on human wishing and "insusceptible of proof" (1964a, p. 31). Thus, Hume and Freud predicted—counterfactually it turns out—that religion would decline sharply in response to advances in education and science. Religion would also diminish as economies moved away from the vicissitudes of agriculture and toward the greater security of advanced, urbanized economies. In Karl Marx's ([1859] 1913) analysis, the forecasted decline of religion is one manifestation of a broader trend toward "modernization."

Economists Corry Azzi and Ronald Ehrenberg (1975) provided a theoretical framework for the secularization hypothesis in their application of the *rational-choice approach* to the demand for religion. A key feature of their model is a link between religiosity and the probability of salvation. This link might reflect perceived effects of religious participation and beliefs—more broadly, "good works" —on the chance of being saved. In contrast to Azzi-Ehrenberg, Martin Luther, the leader of the Protestant Reformation starting in 1517, stressed that a sinner was saved by faith alone, not by works. "Good works," in Luther's theology, consisted of performing one's work through faith. Daily, ordinary work if performed with faith was good: "A good work [is] when a man works at his trade, walks, stands, eats, drinks, sleeps, and does all kinds of works for the nourishment of his body and for the common welfare, and ... God is well pleased with them" (Hart 1995, p. 36). Luther's understanding was that daily activities performed with the proper attitude and motivation were good works.

Luther's contemporary, John Calvin, held a similar view to Luther's, that ordinary, daily activities were to be performed by faith: "God sets more value on the pious management of a household, when the head of it, discarding all avarice, ambition, and other lusts of the flesh, makes it his purpose to serve God in some particular vocation" (Calvin [1541] 1845, 4, XIII, p. 16). This ethic of hard work through faith was complemented by a theology of predestination and the Elect. Often referring to the New Testament book 2 Thessalonians 2:13, Calvin claimed that some were chosen by God to be

FIGURE 2.1. Martin Luther. Workshop of Lucas Cranach the Elder. Harvard Art Museums/ Fogg Museum, Gift of Meta and Paul J. Sachs, 1955.164.

saved while others were not: "Many ... deem it most incongruous that of the great body of mankind some should be predestinated to salvation and others to destruction. The decree, I admit, is dreadful; and yet it is impossible to deny that God foreknew what the end of man was to be before he made him, and foreknew, because he had so ordained by his decree." How would a believer know if he was saved, a member of the Elect? According to Calvin, assurance of salvation was not possible, thereby creating anxieties about whether one had been chosen. Possible signs of salvation were an inward subjective feeling of assurance and concrete blessings from God such as economic success.

In the Azzi-Ehrenberg framework, where religiousness can raise the chance of salvation, there is a clear trade-off between the benefits from religiousness and the time and other costs of greater religious participation. If participation in formal religious services or in individual prayer is a time-intensive activity, as seems reasonable, the prediction—consistent with the secularization view—is that an increase in the value of time—real wages for those working in the formal labor market—reduces this participation. The model implies that time devoted to formal services and personal prayer will be high among persons with low value of time—such as retired persons and women not in the labor force in traditional societies. In addition, older people will spend more time on religion if the probability of salvation depends on cumulated religious activities over one's life. This force is stronger if actions taken late in life count the most for salvation—as is true when past sins can be eradicated through the Catholic Confession or other mechanisms for redemption.[2]

Supply of Religion and the Religion-Market Model

An important supply-side approach is the religion-market model, which follows and elaborates on the thinking of Adam Smith (1791), whose classic work *The Wealth of Nations* is often viewed as the first book in modern economics.[3] The religion-market model argues that government regulation influences competition among religion providers and, thereby, affects the nature of the religion product. Specifically, Smith thought that monopoly providers of religious services tend—as monopolies do generally—to become non-innovative and indolent. This response arose because state religions lacked a strong connection between financial support and the provision of quality service to "customers." Religion, Smith argued, is more vibrant where there is a disassociation between religion and state because the absence of state religion creates a climate for competition among religion providers. Moreover, this competition would generate a great variety of religions available to customers. Thus, Smith's prediction is that a state religion would lower religious participation and, thereby, weaken religious beliefs.

The United States is an example of a country with a free religion market and a great variety of religious offerings. In this pluralistic setting, remarked on by Alexis de Tocqueville in *Democracy in America* ([1835] 2000), competition generates religion "products" that are high in quality and well aligned with individual preferences about degrees of strictness and other characteristics. Participation in formal religious services—and perhaps also levels of religious belief—tend, therefore, to be high.

British sociologist David Martin referred to the United States as the "universality of the experimental model of religion" (1978, p. 31). By this, Martin meant that the United States was founded by dissenting religionists who believed in God above a monarch (King James I) and the ecclesiastical authority of the state church (Church of England). By the time de Tocqueville visited the United States in 1831, John Wesley's Methodism was the largest denomination in the country and was growing rapidly.[4] Methodism preached a universal, attainable salvation that became secularized into the US democratic values of universal inclusion and civil rights. The US model of religion open to all created the conditions necessary for a vibrant religion market. This market featured high participation in formal religious services and high levels of religious belief.

The religion-market model argues that an established state religion—as in the Scandinavian and many other countries—is typically the source of a low degree of religious pluralism and, hence, of low participation in organized religion. However, the connection between pluralism and religious beliefs may be weaker than that between pluralism and attendance at formal services. For example, sociologist Grace Davie (1994) has argued that in post–World War II England—a country in which Anglicanism is the established religion—people have tended over time to curtail participation in formal religion while still maintaining high levels of religious beliefs. Believing relative to belonging can be high, and this pattern was found in our empirical work (discussed in Chapter 3) to encourage economic growth.

Sociologists Mark Chaves and David Cann (1992) extended the religion-market model by developing measures of the extent of state involvement and interference with religious activities.[5] Greater state regulation of religion—which Chaves and Cann gauged by, among other things, whether the government appoints or approves religious leaders—was argued to decrease the efficiency of religion providers and, hence, to generate low rates of attendance.

Historically, governments have attempted to foster religion by restricting secular activities that compete with religious participation. Laws in modern Israel require shops to be closed and alcoholic beverages not to be sold on the Sabbath when Jews traditionally worship. Modern Islamic states have prohibitions on many different types of secular activities. In the United States, legal restrictions, colloquially referred to as "blue laws," on a variety of activities on Sunday are meant to minimize competition with religious worship. Evidence of this effect was found by economists Jonathan Gruber and Daniel Hungerman (2008) in their study of the repeal of blue laws in the United States. Their main sample comprised sixteen US statewide eliminations of blue laws from 1955 to 1991.[6] They found that after a blue law was repealed, religious attendance and religious contributions declined. Using data from the National Longitudinal Survey of Youth, they also found that repealing a blue law resulted in an increase in consumption of alcohol and illicit drugs. These effects were, not surprisingly, concentrated on persons who had previously attended church but had stopped after the blue law was repealed.

Government restrictions on secular activities can also cause an upward shift in the distribution of strictness of religious beliefs and practices. According to Michael McBride (2010), strictness rises because its cost decreases when secular activities are banned. State regulations that prohibit the availability of secular substitutes—such as shopping, attending sports events, driving, or traveling—tend to reinforce a strict religious monopoly. According to McBride, this outcome is typical in many Muslim countries, which highly regulate secular activities.

State religion typically involves subsidies for religious activities, such as paying the salaries of clerics, funding ecclesiastical education, and collecting taxes dedicated to religious purposes. As an example, the Saudi government has subsidized clerics and religious administrators even in foreign countries in an attempt to promote Sunni Islam (see Robert Lacey 2009). Similarly, Iran has been promoting Shia Islam outside its borders. Economic reasoning suggests that these kinds of subsidies would encourage formal religious activity. For example, if the government pays for additional clerics, places of worship, religious education, and the printing of sacred texts, then we would expect to see more employed clerics, more places of worship, more religious schooling, and greater dissemination of religious ideas. More personnel and improved facilities may, in turn, attract more adherents. The point is that, through subsidies, a state religion may have a positive effect on attendance at formal religious services.

The opposite of subsidy is suppression, and some governments have sought to suppress formal religion, either specific ones or in general. Communist countries, such as the Soviet Union, East Germany, and China, tried hard to eradicate organized religion within the public and, to varying degrees, private spheres. A likely reason for this suppression is that organized religion was regarded as competitive politically with the communist quasi-religion (Paul Froese 2008). The former Soviet Union suppressed religion for seventy years to build a nation on Marxist-Leninist ideology that was "scientific" and had a monopoly on truth (Ernest Gellner 1995).

The suppression of the main organized religions by the Soviet government had the unintended consequence of fostering obscure sects and cults (Froese 2008, p. 146). A similar devolution of religion has occurred in communist China since 1949. The suppression and strict regulation of religion by the government has created an underground market for a variety of religious sects and cults (Ian Johnson 2017).

The Chinese government under President Xi Jinping has taken a two-pronged approach to religion. Recognizing the increasing demand for religion in the country since the 1980s, the government, under its national rejuvenation program, favors what it calls the "traditional cultures" of Zen Buddhism, Taoism, Confucianism, and folk religions, while restricting Christianity, Islam, Mahayana Buddhism (Tibet), and Judaism.[7] Borrowing the UNESCO category "intangible cultural heritage," the government has relaxed regulation of folk practices such as fortune tellers, cults to folk deities, healing practices involving herbal remedies, acupuncture, cupping, yoga, Buddhist martial arts, tai chi, and qigong.[8] Viewing traditional religious and spiritual practices as fostering values and morality, the government affirmed them as part of its campaign against corruption.

At the same time that the Chinese government has been promoting "traditional cultures," it has clamped down on Christianity, Islam, and Mahayana Buddhism as "external security threats" to the state. The government, in banning or heavily regulating these religions, is actively seeking to ensure that they do not become native, in the sense of incorporating Chinese cultural customs and practices and developing an indigenous theology (Johnson 2017, p. 328). A major reason the Chinese Communist Party does not want the "sinicization" of these religions is that they have ties to communities of believers overseas. For example, Chinese Protestants are linked with immigrant churches in Canada, Australia, and the United States. Muslims are members of the global *ummah* (religious community) with some participating in the Hajj. The Jewish community in Kaifeng has ties to Israel. The Dalai Lama's government in exile is viewed as a direct threat to Chinese sovereignty over the Tibet Autonomous Region. The Chinese government has sought the eradication of Mahayana Buddhism, particularly the Gelupka sect of which the Dalai Lama is a member (the history of which we explore in Chapter 6).

Recently, China's State Administration for Religious Affairs issued updated regulations on religion that took effect in February 2018. Among these regulations are restrictions that cover Internet discussions of religion, religious education, construction and rental of buildings for religious purposes, and financing and interactions with foreign coreligionists. Although the Chinese government has not issued a white paper on religion since the 1990s, an estimated 67 million Chinese are Protestant and 15 million are Catholic. About half of the estimated 82 million Christians belong to unregistered "house" churches. The World Christian Database estimates that by 2040 Protestants in China will number 450 million. The Communist Party views Protestantism as an uncontrolled mass civic organization and therefore a threat to the party's authority.[9] This threat takes the form of not only perceived foreign influence through the churches, but also Protestant pastors and their congregations openly advocating for freedom of expression and the application of the rule of law to government officials. Given the size of the Christian community, particularly Protestantism, and its broad geographic dispersion in a large country, it is reasonable to assume that the new regulations will be implemented as a deterrent against certain critically outspoken and visible churches rather than an all-out persecution of Christians.

From an empirical perspective, it is interesting to examine not only the impact of communism on participation and religious beliefs but also the changes that occurred after the elimination of communism in many countries in the early 1990s. The question is, if communism disappears, how long does it take for religiosity to return to the level that it would have had if communism had never existed? In the cases of the former Soviet Union and China, religion has rebounded rapidly. The same is true for many former communist countries, with the exception of East Germany. As discussed later, we find that the influence of past communism on religiosity gradually weakens over time.

Long-Term Data on Church Attendance

One way to test the secularization hypothesis is to examine long-term trends in religiosity in an array of countries. However, it is difficult to get long-term information about religious trends because most surveys, such as Gallup in the United States, were not carried out until after World War II. For many countries, good data are missing at least until the 1980s.

Laurence Iannaccone has overcome some of these data problems by making use of information from the International Social Survey Programme (ISSP) to estimate rates of attendance at formal religious services for thirty-one countries back to the 1920s.[10] His insight was to use retrospective questions that asked respondents about how often their mothers and fathers attended church when the respondents were children. In addition, he used questions that asked how often the respondents attended formal religious services when they were age eleven or twelve. Because people of various ages were surveyed by the ISSP in 1991 and 1998, it was possible to use the answers on these surveys to get estimates of church attendance rates back to the 1920s. Also, he got separate estimates for adults (mothers and fathers of the respondents) and children (respondents as children).

For the United States, Iannaccone's numbers on monthly or more church attendance rates show high values that remained fairly flat over time. For example, the rate for adults was 61 percent in 1930 and 55 percent in 1985. For children, the rate was 74 percent in 1930 and 56 percent in 1985. The comparison between the adult and child numbers illustrates two typical facts: church attendance rates tend to be higher for children than for adults, but in many countries the gap has narrowed over time.

There are a few countries in Western Europe that illustrate a clear and pronounced secularization tendency. In France, monthly church attendance rates for adults were 56 percent in 1930 but only 19 percent in 1985. The corresponding numbers for children were 68 and 32 percent. In Germany, monthly church attendance rates for adults were 60 percent in 1930 and 29 percent in 1985, and the corresponding numbers for children were 66 and 41 percent. In Great Britain, the rates for adults were 39 percent in 1930 and 19 percent in 1985, whereas those for children were 77 and 28 percent. Italy also exhibits a substantial decline in church attendance rates for adults, though not as much as for the other three countries. And in Italy the child attendance rates fell by only a small amount from 1930 to 1985.

Scandinavian countries were different in that church attendance rates were low throughout. For example, in Sweden, adult attendance rates were only 19 percent in 1935 and 11 percent in 1985. The corresponding numbers for child attendance rates were 24 and 12 percent. Results for Denmark and Norway were similar. Another place with very low religious participation throughout was Japan. Here the rate for parents was 12 percent in 1930 and 7 percent in 1985. In this case, child rates were similar: 13 percent in 1930 and 7 percent in 1985.

Finally, we can mention two European countries with unusually high church attendance rates over the long term. In Ireland, the adult rate was 98 percent in 1930 and 89 percent in 1985. The corresponding numbers for children were similar: 98 percent in 1930 and 90 percent in 1985.[11] In Poland, adult attendance rates were 85 percent in 1930 and 67 percent in 1985. The corresponding numbers for children were 86 and 81 percent.

If we take all of Iannaccone's data together, we find support for the secularization idea. However, we should not go so far as to conclude that religious participation is rapidly disappearing. And in some rich countries—notably the United States—religious attendance is holding up well.

Recent International Data on Religiosity

We have much more information about religiosity for the period since the 1980s. The data come from international surveys that have now been used by many sociologists and economists. These surveys cover nearly a hundred countries and comprise multiple waves of the World Values Survey or WVS (around 1981, 1990, 1995, 2000, 2005, and 2010) and the ISSP (around 1991, 1998, and 2008).

For attendance at formal religious services, we have information since the 1980s that is much more extensive than that used by Iannaccone. We focused particularly on attendance that was weekly or more and monthly or more. In addition, we have data since the 1980s on the frequency of personal prayer.

There is also extensive information since the 1980s on various religious beliefs, referring for example to heaven and hell and an afterlife or, more broadly, to "god." These concepts are more easily defined in Judeo-Christian contexts but can be extended to other religions, such as achieving perfection in Hinduism and Buddhism. Thus, the data from WVS and ISSP on religious beliefs attempt to cover all countries and religions. We also looked at less specific questions, such as whether people consider themselves to be religious or view religion as important in their lives.

Determinants of Religiosity

We have used the data on religiosity back to the 1980s for nearly one hundred countries to study effects from the level of economic development and other variables. We now discuss the main findings from this research.

SECULARIZATION PATTERNS

Consistent with Iannaccone's long-term data on church attendance, we find a strong negative effect on all measures of religiosity from higher economic development, gauged by real per capita gross domestic product (GDP). This pattern applies to measures of participation that are analogous to the Iannaccone variables—monthly or weekly attendance at formal religious services. The negative relation also holds for measures of religious beliefs—in hell, heaven, an afterlife, and god—and also to whether a person views himself or herself as religious. In this sense, there is strong overall support for the secularization view. This finding is ironic in that scholars advancing the secularization theory have been mostly in retreat over the past couple decades. For example, the sociologist Peter Berger (1996) recanted his earlier stance that favored secularization. In contrast, another sociologist, Rodney Stark (2015), never thought that religion was in retreat.

One observation that boosted the arguments of the non-secularists (such as the sociologists Rodney Stark and Roger Finke) is that the rich United States has maintained high levels of formal religious participation and religious belief over time. Another aspect of the debate is that the secularists, such as Hume and Freud, were unreasonably extreme, arguing counterfactually that religion would rapidly disappear as a significant social force. More accurately, the negative effect from economic development on religiosity is a slow and gradual process.

GOVERNMENT REGULATION OF THE RELIGION MARKET

We examined effects on religiosity from government intervention in the religion market. We focused on two indicators—the presence of a state religion in 1970 and the existence of a form of regulation of the religion market in the 1970s. We discuss in detail our measure of state religion in Chapter 5. The regulation variable, based on Chaves and Cann (1992), is an indicator of whether appointments of church leaders are made by the government or require the approval of the government.

The presence of a state religion is positively related to all of our measures of religiosity. We interpret these patterns as reflecting the subsidies to organized religion that typically accompany a state religion. In contrast, the regulation variable is negatively related to all of our measures of religiosity. We interpret these results in terms of government regulation discouraging competition and leading to lower the quality of religion products.

We also looked at the presence of a communist regime as an extreme case of government regulation of the religion market. In this case, we found clear negative effects from communism on all of our measures of religiosity. These effects tended to dissipate over time once communism had been eliminated, most commonly at the beginning of the 1990s. However, as much as half of the negative effect remained after ten or more years.

We also found interesting patterns of association between religiosity and the form of religious adherence. For attendance at formal religious services, the lowest rates were for Buddhists, Mainline Protestants, Jews, and Hindus. Highest values were for other Christians (mainly evangelicals), Catholics, and Muslims. For religious beliefs, such as in hell and heaven, lowest values were for Mainline Protestants, Buddhists, Hindus, and Jews, and highest values—by far—were for other Christians (evangelicals) and Muslims.

ECONOMIC DEVELOPMENT AND RELIGIOSITY

As mentioned, the overall evidence indicates that richer countries are less religious than poor ones and that religiosity falls as countries get richer. However, to understand this pattern, one has to recognize that economic development is accompanied by a number of changes, including expansions of education, urbanization, and life expectancy. The relation between economic development and religiosity depends on which dimension of development one is talking about.

Education. One argument in the secularization thesis is that people with more formal schooling are more likely to believe in the scientific method and are, therefore, more inclined to reject beliefs that rely on supernatural forces. Put another way, if religious beliefs are based primarily on ignorance, then more educated persons would tend to be less religious. This viewpoint is the one espoused by Hume and Freud.

A contrary argument is that religious beliefs, like many theoretical hypotheses and especially nonverifiable ideas, require abstract thinking. If more educated persons are capable of the abstractions needed for intellectual inquiry, then they may also be more able and willing to make the abstractions needed to support religious beliefs. Therefore, from this perspective, more educated persons may be more religious. Surprisingly, this argument was also made by Freud (1964b), who later in life became more favorably disposed toward religion.

In our empirical analysis, when one holds constant per capita GDP, life expectancy, and urbanization, there is no evidence in the cross-country data that more years of education reduce religiosity. Effects of years of schooling on participation in formal religious services are close to zero, and there is some indication of a positive effect on religious beliefs, particularly those referring to hell and heaven. These results do not sound like the arguments from Hume and the younger Freud that religion is basically irrational.

Perhaps it is not so much the years of school attainment that matter for religiousness but, rather, the quality of the education. Certain religions, such as Judaism, highly value the reading of sacred texts early in life. Consequently, the Jewish religion supported a system of universal primary education (Maristella Botticini and Zvi Eckstein 2012). Jewish learning of the Mishna and Talmud involved reasoning and debating, fostering intellectual curiosity and mental discipline. This interplay accords with a positive relation between education and religious beliefs.

Urbanization. The cross-country data show that all measures of religiosity are strongly inversely related to a country's urbanization rate. In rural areas, participation in religion tends to be markedly higher than in urban areas. Claude Fischer (1978) pointed out that, in cities, organized religion has to compete with many alternative uses of time, such as museums, theaters, shopping, and political participation. Therefore, with urbanization, religious participation becomes only one option among many, and people are less likely to attend formal religious services.

Another possible explanation is that rural dwellers rely on religion to deal with the uncertainties of nature that are particularly important in these areas—for example, those associated with tornadoes, floods, and droughts. The link between the uncertainty of nature and religiosity has been assessed in some recent studies. Daniel Chen (2010) studied the responses of Indonesian households to the economic distress caused by the Asian financial crisis in 1998. He found that greater distress, measured by the fall in per capita consumer expenditure, resulted in higher religious intensity, gauged by Koran study and attendance at Islamic schools. Chen's interpretation is that the financial crisis raised the demand for the type of mutual-aid insurance provided by organized religion. Consistent with this perspective, the impact of economic distress on religiosity was unimportant for households that had ready availability of credit.

Another way to measure religiosity is through popular support for ecclesiastical leaders. Using data from the twelfth century to the fifteenth, Eric Chaney (2013) documented that during periods of unusually high or low Nile flood levels, Egypt's highest ranking religious authority, the *ulamā*, was less likely to be replaced by the sultan, while at the same time expenditures on religious structures increased. During the natural disaster of either the high flooding of the Nile or low water levels, the ulamā extracted greater concessions from the sultan. The explanation is that during a natural disaster, people, including the sultan, sought supernatural intervention with the ulamā as mediator. The real possibility of food riots during a grain shortage (due to either fields flooding or a drought) translated into increased political authority for the ulamā over both the populace and the sultan. The overall conclusion was that an exogenous economic downturn caused by a highly unusual flood level produced economic uncertainty and, thereby, expanded the power of religious leaders.

In a similar vein, Mariano Belloc, Francesco Drago, and Roberto Galbiati (2016) assessed historical effects on religiosity from another form of natural disaster, earthquakes in Italian cities in the middle ages. From 1000 to 1300, many Italian cities changed political institutions from autocracy toward forms of democracy. The authors found that the occurrence of an earthquake made it more likely that religious leaders (bishops) would retain autocratic control of municipalities, as opposed to transitioning to more democratic institutions. The authors' interpretation was that the populace was more inclined to embrace the authority of religious figures when the underlying environment appeared more risky—because of a heightened perceived probability of earthquakes or other natural disasters. These effects arose even when earthquakes did not generate much physical damage—suggesting that the fear of god was more important than any direct effects on stocks of capital or economic activity. Moreover, the effects did not apply to cities headed by autocratic secular leaders, where effects of earthquakes on religiosity would not be relevant. In addition, in cities run by religious authorities, earthquakes tended to raise investments in religious buildings, thereby revealing a direct link between heightened uncertainty and greater religiosity.

In a more recent setting, Christine Binzel and Jean-Paul Carvalho (2017) analyzed the Islamic revival that occurred in Egypt from the mid-1980s through the 1990s. A key factor was the push for widespread educational attainment following the 1952 revolution. Initially, this push was accompanied by expanded employment opportunities that matched the increased human capital. Subsequently, however, employment opportunities for well-educated youth became scarcer, particularly with a decline in the early 1980s in public-sector hiring. Binzel and Carvalho view the Egyptian Islamic revival as a mechanism for coping with these unfulfilled aspirations—sometimes called *relative deprivation*—that is, advanced education not matched by jobs that make good use of this schooling. They argue, specifically, that the Islamic movement—including the rise of the Muslim Brotherhood—was driven by the frustrations of educated youth.

Growth of the Nones

Another approach that researchers have taken toward assessing the secularization hypothesis is to look closely at the growth of nones. The category of "nones" comprises individuals who have no formal religious affiliation, may or may not have a religious education, may hold spiritual beliefs, may be agnostic, or simply cannot decide. Nones may hold general spiritual beliefs, such as belief in God, identify as "spiritual," or be uncommitted or undecided about religion. Nones is a different category from those who believe there is no deity (atheists).

The none category is a growing segment of society around the world, particularly in regions with low fertility and aging populations, such as Europe, North America, China, and Japan (Pew Research Center 2015a). Moreover, as countries grow richer, religious participation by believers declines slightly whereas participation by nonbelievers falls dramatically (see John Huber 2005).

Researchers have found that high scores on three religion questions correlate strongly with whether a person is a strong believer, a *liminal* (a person who sometimes claims to be religious and sometimes to be not religious at all), or a none.[12] These three are belief in God, belief that the Bible (or analogous sacred text) is the literal word of God, and extent of attendance at formal religious services. Those who score high on these questions tend to be strong believers, whereas those who score low tend to be nones. Those who score in between—the liminals—are neither committed to organized religion nor committed to a denial of religion. Michael Hout (2017) estimates from recent data that 70 percent of Americans consistently have a religious affiliation, 10 percent never had one, and 20 percent sometimes do and sometimes don't (liminal). These results mean that one in five Americans can be described as a liminal.

The overwhelming majority of nones were brought up in a religious tradition. This finding by the Pew Research Center is confirmed by Hout and Claude Fischer (2014), who found that those with an upbringing in a religious tradition were increasingly less likely to state a religious preference in adulthood, compared to people in earlier cohorts. As an example, the comedian Pete Holmes was raised and formally educated as an evangelical Protestant. In his late twenties, Holmes began to question the religion he was raised and educated in for the first twenty-two years of his life. He explored other options, including Buddhism, and today Holmes self-identifies as being an unaffiliated "Christ-leaning spiritual seeker."[13] Like many of the unaffiliated, Holmes is no longer willing to restrict his religious options to one faith. This type of religiosity has been colloquially called "religion a la carte." Many unaffiliated are seeking the spiritual fulfillment that one religion may be unable to provide. They pick and choose beliefs, and this can be within one religious tradition or more than one.

The percentage of Americans who were raised without a religious affiliation is rising gradually, from about 3 percent in the early 1970s to about 8 percent in the past decade (Pew Research Center

2012b). Roughly 40 percent of those raised without a religion continued to be nonreligious as adults, a third were liminal, and a quarter were committed to religion (Hout 2017). Among people born between 1981 and 1996 (Millennials) and raised with religion, 22 percent preferred no religion in 2012. This percentage is 50 percent higher than that for people born twenty years earlier and five times that for those born fifty years earlier. As they grow older, the percentage of Millennials who are nones is likely to rise.

These patterns fit with findings by Hout and Fischer (2014) for earlier times. They found that US individuals raised in the 1960s were more likely to prefer no religion in adulthood than were people raised with no religion prior to the 1960s. For example, among people born in the 1960s and raised without religion, 60 percent preferred no religion in adulthood; among people who were born in the 1930s and raised without religion, only 24 percent had no religious preference when they were interviewed as adults.

Nones and Religiosity at Harvard University

We got a more personal perspective on the secularization hypothesis and the role of nones by asking students in 2015 and 2017 in our "Religion and Political Economy" class at Harvard to conduct surveys on religion at their undergraduate houses. One finding was that around 40 percent of students were nones or atheists. These students were at the tail end of Millennials, born in the 1990s. The Millennials make up the largest group of nones in the United States (35 percent in 2015), and our inference from the Harvard survey is that many of these undergraduate nones were raised by parents who did not affiliate with a formal religion or provide their children with a religious education.

These results correspond to those from a survey of incoming freshmen by the college newspaper, the *Harvard Crimson* (2015). The fraction that classified themselves as "not at all religious" ranged from 31 to 34 percent for incoming classes between 2013 and 2017. Those self-labeling as not at all or not very religious ranged between 57 and 60 percent.

Harvard has often been described as "godless," which is ironic given that in 1636 the college was founded to educate Congregational (Puritan) ministers.[14] Given this recent reputation for godlessness, one would expect that a four-year education at Harvard would have a secularizing influence on the religious beliefs and participation of its undergraduates. By secularization, we mean a decline in personal religious beliefs and practices as well as a weakening in identification with organized religion. In fact, this is not the case. Our survey findings showed that students without a religious identity typically entered Harvard in that status. Our results did not show a substantial decline in identification with organized religion or in religious beliefs while attending Harvard. Thus, it is wrong to conclude that Harvard is having a secularizing influence on its undergraduates; rather there is something about Harvard—presumably along with similar top universities—that tends to attract nonreligious people.

Our results were consistent with a survey conducted among Harvard undergraduates in 1959 by Parker Rossman and colleagues (1960). Similar to students surveyed in 2015 and 2017, Harvard undergraduates in 1959 tended to believe in God without associating that belief with any detailed doctrine, but, rather, in a generic way as a permeating "presence." Students were more spiritual than religious in the sense that they formulated their own amalgam of beliefs. Agnosticism was prevalent among the respondents, with God being described as "a vast, impersonal principle of order or natural uniformity." Liminals showed up in the survey as well, with 85 percent of the agnostic respondents stating that they could not deny God's existence any more than they could affirm it.

The surveyors of 1959 concluded that students typically entered Harvard with these belief characteristics, with religious changes more likely to occur in secondary school than in college. Entering students embodied the secularizing of American society, which viewed higher education as the "institutional center for developing the knowledge on which modern technological society depends" (Joe Nichols 2017, p. 171). As Rossman et al. (1960, p. 30) put it, "It would appear from this survey that Harvard is not to a significant extent altering the morals and ethics of students, although it may be inferred that Harvard has more influence upon political opinions than upon religious opinions. Harvard students do become liberal."

This last finding from the 1959 survey conflicts with recent evidence. In 2017, students tended to enter Harvard as liberal—about 70 percent of incoming students described themselves this way. Specifically, 88 percent had an unfavorable opinion of President Donald Trump, whereas 86 percent had a favorable opinion of former president Barack Obama. Harvard did not seem to be having a liberalizing effect on students. Rather, students entered the college already identifying as liberals. This pattern accords with the broader pattern in which Millennials have the highest percentage of Democratic identification (55 percent), compared with the previous generation, in which 27 percent identified as Democrats (Pew Research Center 2017a).

Religious Conversion

Although most people remain in the religion in which they were brought up, there are many people who change their religion during their lifetimes. For example, Michael Marissen (2016, p. xv), a scholar of J. S. Bach's music, described his religious upbringing as Dutch Calvinist. Later in life he chose to become a Methodist, moved on to Reconstructionist Judaism, and more recently shifted to agnosticism. We think of the process of choosing a religion (even if it is the same one in which we were raised) as voluntary and involving rational choice; that is, we apply the same kind of framework that we use to understand attendance at formal religious services. However, the conversion process can be influenced by constraints imposed by governments or organized religions.

CONCEPTUAL FRAMEWORK

Suppose that, at a given point in time, a person has preferences about the characteristics and services offered by alternative religions.[15] For example, some religions are stricter than others, and people have varying preferences about strictness. Suppose further that a person can choose among a set of religions that are currently available in her location. Typically, only a few religions have sufficient representation in a person's neighborhood to be attractive—because they can offer shared experiences with other adherents, provide formal religious services and religious training for children, and so on.

The switch from one's current faith to an alternative tends to be costly, for example, if there are legal restrictions on conversion or if an alternative religion is unfamiliar. These costs of conversion may include becoming an outcaste (apostate) as well as being excluded from one's previously formed religious and social networks. However, we assume that a change in religion is feasible at some cost. Not surprisingly, the higher this cost, the lower the propensity to convert.

Given the cost of converting, the tendency to switch will be greater when the alternative religion is more attractive compared to one's incumbent religion. Usually, young people who are influenced by their parents will value their current religion highly, but life-cycle changes (including marrying someone of another faith) may create a gap between an alternative and the current status. For example, with the dramatic growth of evangelical Protestantism, many adherents to Mainline Protestantism became more attracted by this alternative. In general, greater pluralism of religious representation in a country or region means better religious alternatives for the typical person and, therefore, a higher rate of religious conversion.

The cost of not adhering to one's most favored religion depends on how important formal religion is to a person. For example, if one cares little about religion in general, it will typically not be worth the trouble to make a change. As an example, communist regimes, notably in East Germany and the Soviet Union, tried hard to diminish the value that people attached to religious participation and beliefs. To the extent that this influence on people's values persisted after the demise of communism (in most countries in the early 1990s), there would be a continuing negative influence of past communism on religious conversion.

Some researchers, including Ed Glaeser and Bruce Sacerdote (2008), argue that one of the benefits of religion is its social networking role. These benefits tend to be greater for more educated persons. Through this channel, greater education will raise the benefits of having one's "correct" religion and, thereby, promote religious conversion.

As already mentioned, the propensity to change religion depends on the costs of making a switch. Some of these costs reflect outside restrictions. For example, most Muslim countries have prohibitions or restrictions on moving out of the Islamic faith or on switching from other religions into Islam. Some countries, including non-Muslim ones, have restrictions on proselytizing or intermarriage, activities that interact closely with religious conversion. A general prediction is that greater restrictions on conversion will reduce the observed rate of religious conversion.

At an individual level, one important determinant of the costs of changing religion is education. More educated people likely find it easier to change religions because they are better at learning and adjusting to new ways of thinking. Greater education tends also to go along with more information about alternative religions and with greater contact with people of other faiths. We therefore predict that higher education results in more religious conversion—the effect on reduced costs of conversion reinforces the previously discussed effect on the benefits of having the right religion.

We discussed before the typical secularization pattern, whereby higher real per capita GDP goes along with reduced demand for religion, gauged by attendance at formal religious services and religious beliefs. From this perspective, we might predict that higher per capita GDP would lower religious conversion. However, reduced participation in formal religious services or beliefs does not necessarily mean that people lower their spending on religion, and this spending will measure the value placed overall on religion. Since higher income goes along with more spending (on religion and other things), the overall effect of per capita GDP on religious conversion is ambiguous.

In an earlier study, we analyzed the empirical determinants of religious conversion for forty countries by using information provided by the ISSP and the WVS. We used responses from these surveys (ISSP 1991 and 1998 and WVS 2001) on two questions:

What religion do you adhere to currently?

What religion did you adhere to as a child (age 11 or 12)?

We took as our sample persons who were currently at least thirty—because we knew from the General Social Survey (GSS) religion module of 1988 that most religious conversions occurred before that age.[16]

We classified the answers in each case into eight broad types of religions—Catholic, Protestant, Islam, Hindu, Eastern religions (including Buddhist), Jewish, Orthodox, and Other—and a category of no religion (including atheists). Thus, our data allowed us to detect whether a person had changed religion—that is, converted—at least once since childhood and up to the present date (for persons currently at least thirty). In our analysis, we did not consider shifts to or from no religion as constituting a conversion. And we did not count as conversions movements within major groups, notably among types of Protestantism or Islam. We then computed the number of conversions—that is, the number who had a different religion at age thirty and above compared with that as a child.[17] The conversion rate was then the ratio of this number to the number of persons who adhered to some religion as a child.

One shortcoming of the available data is that they include a breakdown among forms of Christianity—Catholic, Protestant, and Orthodox (with Anglican included as Protestant)—but not among types of Muslims or other major groups. The lack of breakdown among types of Muslims did not matter much for our analysis because the questions that allowed the computation of conversion rates were not asked in countries that were predominantly Muslim (by the WVS, which covered many Muslim-majority countries). Probably the question about growing up in a different religion was not asked because inquiring about this possibility would be regarded as insulting in Muslim countries. In addition, the Pew Research Center (2012a) reported that switches between the two major forms of Islam—Sunni and Shia—were rare.

Among the forty countries for which we have data, those with conversion rates above 10 percent are Canada, the United States, New Zealand, and Chile. Those with convergence rates below 1 percent are Finland, Romania, Slovenia, Bulgaria, Spain, Italy, Hungary, the Slovak Republic, Cyprus, and Poland.

Empirically, the most important determinant of the rate of religious conversion is a country's religious diversity, which depends inversely on the fraction of the adhering population that belongs to the most popular religion. Places with substantial religious representation outside of the main religion—such as Canada, Switzerland, Germany, the Netherlands, the United States, and Australia—tend to have many religious conversions. Places that are dominated by a single religion—such as the Scandinavian countries, Spain, Belgium, Poland, Japan, Italy, Slovenia, and Portugal—tend to have little religious conversion.

Greater education, measured by years of school attainment, turns out to increase the conversion rate. This result accords with our theoretical reasoning, whereby more education lowers the cost of converting and also raises the benefit from having the "right" religion. In contrast, for given education, the conversion rate turns out to be independent of the level of economic development, measured by real per capita GDP. This result is consistent with the theory, in the sense that the predicted effect from per capita GDP was ambiguous.

We found that, other things equal, a history of communism (gauged by presence around 1970) led to a lower rate of religious conversion. In our sample, this communist history applied to six countries that were formerly part of the Soviet Union and eight that were in Eastern Europe (two of which had been part of Yugoslavia).

To measure legal restrictions on religious conversion, we used information from Jonathan Fox (2018). He provides information for 1990 to the present on four measures of these restrictions. The first applies to conversion into minority religions, the second to conversion out of the majority religion, the third to proselytizing, and the fourth to interfaith marriage. However, none of the forty countries in our sample had legal restrictions of the first two forms. These direct restrictions on religious conversion typically prevail in predominantly Muslim countries—among thirty-nine countries with Islamic adherence of at least 50 percent, Fox (2018) shows that twenty-five have conversion restrictions either out of the majority religion or into a minority religion, and eighteen have both types of restrictions. As already mentioned, our sample does not include any of these predominantly Muslim countries. Therefore, in our analysis, we measured legal restrictions on religious conversion only by whether a country had in place (around 1990) restrictions on proselytizing or interfaith marriage. These restrictions applied to ten countries in our sample. We found empirically that the presence of these restrictions reduced the rate of religious conversion.

We found that a number of other variables were not significantly related to religious conversion. For example, conversion was not related to two variables discussed earlier in this chapter: the presence of a state religion or regulation of the religion market (gauged by whether the government appointed or approved religious leaders). Conversion was also not related to the extent of religious participation and beliefs, variables also described earlier. Finally, the composition of religious adherence was mostly unimportant, except for a small negative effect from the Islamic adherence share. Possibly this share reveals restrictions on conversion that were not adequately captured by the variable we were able to measure.

DETERMINANTS OF RELIGIOSITY

We showed in this chapter the complexities of the determination of religiosity. As the ability of researchers to carry out international surveys and analyze the resulting data has improved, we have gained a better understanding of how religion responds to economic development and to government regulation and subsidy. We found support for the secularization hypothesis, which states that as societies grow richer, they tend to reduce participation in formal religious services, religious beliefs such as in hell and heaven, and the role of religion in political decision making. We found that government regulation of the religion market tended to reduce competition and, thereby, tended to lower religious participation and beliefs. However, a state religion could raise religiousness, partly by subsidizing organized religion and partly by restricting secular alternatives, such as attending sporting events on Sundays.

When discussions of declines in religious beliefs and attendance in industrialized societies became a hot topic in the 1960s, the term "secularization" was treated as the opposite of "religiosity." We now understand that the term refers to a variety of phenomena, the least of which is the disappearance of religion. As part of dealing with this varied spiritual experience, scholars have invented new categories such as "nones" and "liminals" to more finely capture changes in religious believing and belonging within the context of economic development. People are choosing their religious beliefs (a la carte religion) with little regard for doctrinal orthodoxy, thereby making the religion market more fluid.

China is a particularly interesting place in which to examine further the interaction between religion and political economy. China's diverse population with majority Han representation is increasingly attracted by formal religion, notably variants of evangelical Protestantism. This attraction reflects the global nature of evangelicalism and the increased drive by individuals and the government to achieve a clearer moral compass. Notably, religion may turn out to be helpful in dealing with widespread corruption in China. Important questions concern whether it is the introduction of capitalist ideas and policies in China since the late 1970s that made evangelicalism more attractive and whether China will continue to deregulate the religion market as it economically liberalizes.

A second underinvestigated topic for future study is the devolution of religion that occurs under harsh state suppression of religion. The banning of religious texts, rituals, and education translates into a generational loss of knowledge regarding doctrines, beliefs, and practices. Without a community of believers and religious leaders to pass on knowledge, ignorance of what constitutes one's faith and what makes one's faith unique leads to mistaken assumptions. Religious capital, like other types of human capital, if not acquired leads to ignorance. This gives rise to "atypical" or "creative cross-cultural" adaptations of religious beliefs and ideas.

In the next chapter, we look at religion as an independent variable, that is, as a causal influence on economic growth and other outcomes. A key issue here is how religiosity affects economic performance partly by altering individual characteristics—such as work ethic, honesty, and thrift—and partly by influencing education and, thereby, the accumulation of productive human capital.

Religion and Economic Growth

As mentioned in Chapter 2, a famous argument for why religion stimulates economic growth comes from the German sociologist Max Weber ([1904–1905] 1930) in his *Protestant Ethic and the Spirit of Capitalism*. In Weber's vision, religious beliefs affect the economy primarily by fostering character traits such as work ethic, honesty (and hence trust), and thrift. He thought that these traits—stimulated by the Protestant Reformation of the 1500s—contributed to the Industrial Revolution from the 1700s to the mid-1800s. He argued that this linkage explains why this revolution took off earlier in Protestant areas, such as England, parts of Germany, and the Netherlands, rather than in Catholic ones, such as France and Italy.

A key point about religion in the Weberian framework is that religious beliefs are what matter for economic outcomes. This approach contrasts with a social-capital perspective, in which the networking associated with attendance at formal religious services could be growth promoting. This alternative view may not take religion sufficiently seriously in that it regards participation in formal religion as just one of many ways to build social capital or to form a communal culture. For Weber, houses of worship were not primarily another kind of social club. The special feature of religion is its potential for instilling beliefs that reinforce important traits and values, in other words, the accumulation of a type of human capital.

Salvation and World Religions

We take the position that religion is sui generis. Otherworldly compensators (salvation, damnation, nirvana) are great motivators of behavior in this world. The major religions of the world—Hinduism, Buddhism, Islam, and Christianity—exhibit beliefs in salvation that link in differing ways to economic incentives.[1]

A key concept is what we call salvific merit, which connects the perceived probability of salvation to a person's lifetime activities. In some religions, salvific merit can be earned in this life to enhance the chances of a better outcome in the next life (salvation, damnation). Religions with high salvific merit, such as Buddhism, give believers an array of worldly opportunities to spiritually advance, for example, acquiring wealth honestly and using it to support the *Sangha* (community of monks), giving offerings, and showing generosity toward family and friends. Religions with medium salvific merit, such as Hinduism, Catholicism, and Islam, offer moderate opportunities for earning spiritual advancement in this life. Complementing these limited opportunities are the equally important chances to pay off one's sins or wrongdoings. Finally, religions with low or zero chances of earning salvific merit, such as Protestantism, view human action as having no impact on attaining salvation or damnation.

This analytical model of salvific merit illustrates that beliefs in otherworldly compensators can raise productivity by fostering individual traits such as honesty, work ethic, and thrift. In other contexts, the powerful force from afterlife beliefs can promote antisocial actions, including violence—the so-called "dark side of religion."

In Christianity, particularly Protestantism, the emphasis is on individual intention and responsibility for religious obligations. Religious beliefs in Protestantism create an individualistic approach to otherworldly compensators and a focus on personal accountability to God. In contrast, Islam tends to be legalistic and communitarian, stressing the fulfillment not only of religious obligations but also of social and political responsibilities shared by being a member of the ummah (religious community). As the Qur'an lays out the prophet Muhammad's conception of the ummah and individual responsibility within it, the idea of *fitna* (temptation and distress) maintains communal harmony by condemning actions or thoughts that might cause dissention, conflict, rebellion, or temptation.[2]

Shari'a in Islam, unlike Christianity and particularly Protestantism, is a corpus of religious law focused on orthopraxy (correct conduct) through the application of religious principles to daily life. The ulamā (learned scholars) identified religious activities that cultivated this Shari'a-mindedness as the major organizing principle of Islam (Bryan Turner 2010). Lawrence Rosen (2000) argues that, in Islam's worldview, transgression is equated with social harm. The reasoning is that a transgression might easily give rise to conflict, in which doubts about one's beliefs result in social chaos.

A more fundamental aspect of human agency in Islam highlights its difference from Protestantism. In Islam, the nature of external evidence determines the intentionality and social harm caused by a transgression. A mistake, for example, speaking ill of someone in a public space without being aware that others are within hearing range, is viewed as an intentional wrongdoing, not one due to carelessness or emotional outburst. The logic is that "no competent person would engage in such a public assertion if he did not mean what he said" (Rosen 2000, p. 192).[3] Leaving unpunished such accidental behavior opens the possibility for harm to the orderliness of the ummah. Thus, in Islam, the paramount value of the religious-social cohesion of a properly ordered ummah is embedded in what to the Western mind is a legalistic interpretation of human action.

We think that the social-capital and cultural aspects of religion—communal services, rituals, religious schools—are significant mainly to the extent that they influence beliefs and, hence, behavior. For given beliefs, more time spent on communal activities would tend to be an economic drag for the believer as well as the entire community. Moreover, the costs of formal religion include the time spent by adherents and religious officials on religious activities. In addition, time and money are expended on buildings, sacred objects, and so on. Our general view, based on empirical evidence that we discuss later, is that believing relative to belonging (attending) is the main channel through which religion matters for economic and other social outcomes.

Ideas from the Protestant Reformation

MARTIN LUTHER

Weber discussed Martin Luther, who began the Reformation in 1517 supposedly by posting his ninety-five theses on the door of the All Saints' Church in Wittenberg, Germany.[4] Luther's document constituted an attack on an array of corrupt religious practices, such as selling indulgences and church offices, which had contributed to the vast accumulation of wealth by the Catholic Church. Although Luther did not want to leave the Church and create an alternative religion, he did argue forcefully for drastic reforms. Not surprisingly, the Catholic hierarchy reacted to Luther and his followers with sharp antagonism, leading to the Catholic Counter-Reformation, as embodied in the Council of Trent from 1545 to 1563. This antagonism led to a long period of religious-based warfare, culminating in 1648 with the Peace of Westphalia at the end of the devastating Thirty Years' War.

In terms of theology related to economic incentives, Luther stressed the concept of "the calling," a divine ordinance that prescribed a person's obligations in the material world. Luther, similar to some of his medieval contemporaries, interpreted the calling as referring to the socioeconomic conditions into which one was born and against which it was sinful to rebel. The specific form of the calling varied across persons, consistent with the efficient division of labor in society (an idea pursued later and more cogently by Adam Smith [1791] in *The Wealth of Nations*).[5] Most importantly, Luther's approach looked favorably on hard work and material success and did not advocate the monastic ascetic lifestyle embraced by the Catholic Church. One's faith informed everything one did, day in and day out. "As you live, you shall fare." Through observing people's behavior, according to Luther, we can perceive if they are acting in faith or have no faith. Because Luther brought asceticism into daily living, his teachings were unclear about the individual incentives to follow one's calling. Important here is that Luther specifically rejected the notion of "good works," whereby people could enhance their chances of salvation in the next world by engaging in satisfactory behavior in this world.

JOHN CALVIN AND PREDESTINATION

According to Weber, "Although the Reformation is unthinkable without Luther's own personal religious development, and was spiritually long influenced by his personality, without Calvinism his work could not have had permanent concrete success." Therefore, Weber ([1904–1905] 1930, pp. 89–90) said, "We, thus, take as our starting point in the investigation of the relationship between the ... Protestant ethic and the spirit of capitalism the works of Calvin."

Luther, but Calvin much less, believed that God's purpose for humans was work. Thus, as in Aristotle (1941, NE 1.7, 1097b22–23), "For just as for a flute-player, a sculptor, or an artist, and, in general, for all things that have a function or activity, the good and the 'well' is thought to reside in the function, so it would seem to be for man, if he has a function." Calvin shared Luther's idea that the world was theologically ordered by a Christian God, but they differed on the nature of the function of humans. Luther's Protestantism posited human function as working every day at what one was called by God to do. Luther thought that the profession one was born into—a tanner, blacksmith, bookkeeper—was one's proper station in life. Moral and religious good coincided with performing one's daily work in this designated area. Should we choose not to work, we become indolent, giving into bodily urges and physical pleasures, becoming restless, mentally unfocused, and lacking in discipline, and thereby engaging in "folly and rashness." Although Luther and Calvin agreed with this view, their theologies diverged on the practical implications of work. Whereas Luther viewed work (one's calling) as maintaining political stability and socioeconomic order, Calvin argued that work gave each person "stability and order" (Ernst Troeltsch [1931] 1992, pp. 641–650). Thus, in contrast to Luther, mobility and the pursuit of a better position were acceptable in Calvin's thinking, if done for the right reasons. The idea of improving the quality of one's circumstances through work, including changing professions if necessary, was part of God's calling and the godly society.[6] Consistent with this reasoning, Calvin was instrumental in introducing the textile industry in Geneva to employ the poor and idle (p. 642). Economic prosperity and moral rectitude were intertwined with profits from that labor as blessings from God.

A key element in Calvin's thinking is the doctrine of predestination. The idea is that an elect group of individuals were chosen by God for divine grace. For others, no morally worthy actions in this world can lead to salvation. However, a person cannot know with anything close to certainty whether he or she is one of the elect group. Moreover, people cannot tell whether other persons are in or out.

At first glance, predestination would seem to cut strongly against individual incentives to work hard, save, behave ethically, and so on. Instead, this fatalistic theology would seem to encourage laziness and low productivity. After all, if salvation were preordained, why bother to work hard and behave well in this life? Or, at least, the motivation for material success and good behavior must come only from rewards in this life—a religious connection related to salvation would not exist.

However, Calvin ([1563] 1845) turned this reasoning around by arguing that people sought signs that they had been chosen by God. Thus, according to Weber ([1904–1905] 1930), "However useless good works might be as a means of attaining salvation ... they are indispensable as a sign of election." The point is that material success is a sign of God's approval and thus of one's election. Hence, the incentive for hard work and accumulation of wealth derives from the perceived connection between material success and God's approval. Although one cannot achieve complete certainty about

one's salvation, one can get signs that make the perceived probability of salvation higher or lower.

Calvin argued that God demands of each person a lifetime of
good works that are performed according to a morality derived
from revealed theology.[7] Only by living a morally good life in this
world could one relieve the psychological uncertainty called "salvation anxiety," never knowing whether one will be saved. Contrary to
the Catholic ascetic view that allowed for the continual cycle of
"sin, repentance, atonement, release, and sin again," Calvinist Protestantism required faith and daily moral conduct as the means of
assuaging salvation anxiety.[8] In Calvin's ([1563] 1845, p. 472) words,
"When we stress that faith ought to be certain and secure, we do
not have in mind a certainty without doubt or a security without
any anxiety. Rather, we affirm that believers have a perpetual struggle with their own lack of faith, and are far from possessing a peaceful conscience, never interrupted by any disturbance."

Salvation anxiety explains the convergence of religiously driven
motivation and economic productivity. A person can never have
epistemological certainty that he is saved but can gain confidence
and counteract "feelings of religious anxiety" through achievements
in this world (Weber [1904–1905] 1930, p. 67). Only through the
daily exercise of self-discipline and methodical hard labor could an
individual find some psychological peace.

R. H. Tawney (1936, pp. 230–231) described this individual
psychological motivation in terms of social moral approbation.
Poverty was "not a misfortune to be pitied and relieved, but a moral
failing to be condemned," and wealth was "the blessing which rewards the triumph of energy and will." Salvation anxiety motivates
people to be productive, but more importantly, to be successful in
their labors.

JOHN WESLEY AND METHODISM

Weber also cites the ideas of John Wesley, the founder of Methodism in England in the mid-1700s. Wesley (1978, pp. 124–136) fa-
mously urged his congregants in 1760 to "gain all you can, save all

you can, give all you can." Thus, his first two precepts support the pursuit of material success in this life. Not only did Wesley's theology allow for a role for good works, he also argued that a believer could have salvific assurance. Specifically, Wesley's thinking seems better than Calvin's predestination argument for providing individual motivation for economic success.

Wesley expressed regret that he had been more successful with his congregants in pushing his first two tenets—gaining and saving—than in the third, which advocated giving. He observed (Wesley 1978, pp. 258–261) that, as his congregants became richer, they became less devout, thus giving an early expression of the secularization hypothesis, which we discussed in the previous chapter: "Religion must necessarily produce both industry and frugality, and these cannot but produce riches. But as riches increase, so will pride, anger, and love of the world.... So, although the form of religion remains, the spirit is swiftly vanishing away. Is there no way to prevent this—this continual decay of pure religion?"

We can appreciate Wesley's despair. Disciplined labor and profit motivation led to the triumph of capitalism. From the standpoint of promoting economic growth, Wesley's first two tenets—work ethic and thrift—are more important than the third, which concerns private charity. Wesley despaired over the weakening ability of religion to "bind business within the discipline of Christian justice and charity" (Hector Robertson 1959, pp. 210–211). In other words, the motivational dimension of the concept of a calling—to work hard for God's approval—changed as the spirit of capitalism gained in popularity.

Consistent with Wesley's secularization view, Weber thought that the Protestant Reformation was important for economic success during the Industrial Revolution (say through the mid-1800s) but not in his own time of the late nineteenth and early twentieth centuries: "Today ... any relationship between religious beliefs and conduct is generally absent, and where any exists, at least in Germany, it tends to be of a negative sort. The people filled with the spirit of capitalism today tend to be indifferent, if not hostile, to the Church.... Religion appears to them as a means of drawing people away from labour in this world" (Weber [1904–1905] 1930, p. 70).

The secularization of society led to increasing emphasis on individual achievement and involvement in profit-making activity at the same time that religion-based morality was declining. Tawney (1936) argued that when religious beliefs, which once morally restricted economic activity, lost their relevance (for whatever reasons) to people's lives, the acquisition of wealth as an end in itself became acceptable. In particular, once modern capitalism was established—possibly with the support of Protestantism in some countries—the subsequent economic success led to attitudes about work and profit that no longer depended on religious beliefs.

Despite Max Weber's doubts about the continuing connection between religion and productivity, we have carried out research with twentieth- and twenty-first-century data related to the Weberian hypothesis that some forms of religious beliefs encourage economic growth. We think this type of research is interesting and important even though Weber would not have staked the success or failure of his theory about the Protestant work ethic on the link between religiosity and economic growth in the twentieth and twenty-first centuries. In fact, Weber would have predicted no important relationship in this period.

Religion and Economic Growth in Modern Data

Since the 1990s, starting with Robert Barro (1991), there has been substantial cross-country empirical research seeking to understand the major determinants of economic growth. This work builds on the conceptual framework of the *neoclassical growth model*, developed particularly by Robert Solow (1956).[9] Much of the empirical work has focused on the period since 1960, where there are data for around one hundred countries on economic growth, gauged by real per capita GDP and an array of other economic, political, and social variables.

In empirical growth studies, the important explanatory variables include the level of per capita GDP at some initial date (such as 1960), aspects of human capital (education and health), the saving rate, openness to international trade, and the government's fiscal and monetary policies. However, an important finding from this research is that explaining economic growth requires an extension beyond narrow economic variables to include measures of the po-' litical and institutional environment. Important forces that have been isolated include maintenance of the rule of law and democracy and the extent of official corruption.

Other researchers argue that economic growth depends on a nation's culture and that religion is an important part of this culture. This perspective fits with Weber's argument that, at least in some circumstances, religious beliefs influence characteristics such as work effort and thrift and, thereby, affect economic growth. Therefore, our empirical strategy for explaining economic growth, implemented in Robert Barro and Rachel McCleary (2003), added measures of religious beliefs and participation to existing empirical frameworks, which included an array of economic, political, and institutional variables.

We collected information about religious beliefs and attendance at formal religious services from two well-known international surveys that we discussed in Chapter 2: the World Values Survey (WVS) and the International Social Survey Programme (ISSP). (For the United States, the General Social Survey or GSS is part of the ISSP.) The WVS has been carried out in six waves since 1981, and the ISSP in three waves since 1991.

One advantage of the WVS is that it has broad coverage across the world: ninety-eight places (mostly countries) have participated at least once in its six surveys. The latest wave, covering 2010–2014, surveyed fifty-nine places. The sample, therefore, goes beyond rich Christian countries to include twenty-six predominantly Muslim countries, many nations in Latin America and Asia, and several countries in sub-Saharan Africa. In contrast, the ISSP's three surveys have reached only forty-one countries. This sample focuses on the OECD (the Organisation for Economic Co-operation and Development, which is basically a rich countries' club), along with representation in Eastern Europe, Latin America, and parts of Asia. The sample includes only one predominantly Muslim country (Turkey) and only one country in Africa (South Africa). Due partly to its targeting of richer countries with better institutions, the data from the ISSP are more reliable than those from the WVS. But there is a trade-off of better quality data in the ISSP against a much more restricted sample. For carrying out empirical research, it makes sense to combine information from the ISSP and WVS.

Our study focuses on religious beliefs related to an afterlife, particularly about hell and heaven. In terms of motivations for "good behavior," we think of hell as the stick and heaven as the carrot. Our measure of belief in hell or heaven is the fraction of the population that responds yes to the question of whether they hold this belief. The surveys included these questions for all countries and religions because they went beyond the familiar notions of eternal life stressed in Christianity and Islam. For example, in Hinduism and Buddhism, the concepts relate to reincarnation, accumulating good karma, and achieving perfection. In contrast to beliefs in hell and heaven, survey answers to questions concerning belief in "God" or a general posture of being religious did not relate significantly to economic growth.

In terms of religious participation, our analysis focuses on the fraction of the population that participates in formal services at least monthly. We call this variable "church attendance," but the forms and locations of religious services differ across countries and types of religions. The results for weekly church attendance turn out to be similar to those for monthly attendance.

Figure 3.1 gives the flavor of the empirical results. These results apply for given values of a list of explanatory variables that includes the initial level of per capita GDP, measures of human capital and the quality of institutions, saving rates, and so on. The upper panel shows that, for given belief in hell, an increase in monthly church attendance leads to a decline in economic growth. The lower panel shows that, for given church attendance, an increase in belief in hell leads to an increase in economic growth. Overall, what mostly counts for religion's effect on economic growth seems to be believing (for example, in hell) relative to belonging (for example, to a church).[10]

The effect from religious belief in the lower panel of the figure relates to the channel posited by Max Weber. If greater belief in hell

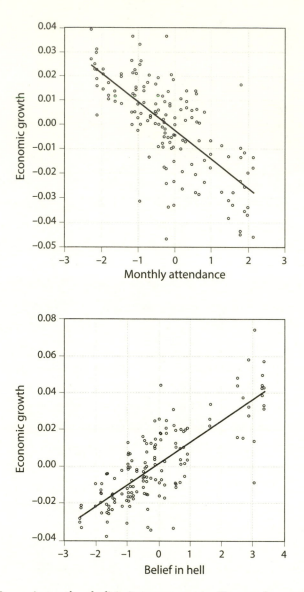

FIGURE 3.1. Economic growth and religiosity across countries. These results come from Robert Barro and Rachel McCleary (2003). (Results are similar when the data are updated to incorporate more recent information.) On the vertical axes, the world average of economic growth (2.2 percent per year) corresponds to 0.00. A rise or fall by 0.01 means that the growth rate is increased or decreased by 1 percentage point per year. On the horizontal axes, the value 0 means that the variable takes on its world average value, which is 32 percent for monthly church attendance and 37 percent for belief in hell. The scaling used is roughly proportionate, that is, corresponding to percentage changes in attendance or belief. The value 1 on the horizontal axes means that monthly church attendance is 57 percent, whereas belief in hell is 61 percent. The value −1 means that monthly church attendance is 15 percent, whereas belief in hell is 17 percent.

encourages people to perform "better," and if this improvement means enhanced work effort, thrift, honesty, and so on, then it makes sense that economic growth would rise. We get basically similar results if we replace belief in hell by belief in heaven. However, if we consider the two beliefs at the same time, the results suggest that belief in hell counts more. That is, the stick from hell seems to work better than the carrot from heaven.

In the upper panel of Figure 3.1, the negative effect on growth from higher participation in formal religious services makes sense if we think of the religion sector's principal output as religious beliefs. Church attendance is then one of the key inputs to the religion sector. If attendance rises—for given religious beliefs—the religion sector must be less productive. In other words, beliefs fall when expressed relative to the time spent in church. From this perspective, it seems reasonable that the larger drain on resources from more time devoted to formal religion would impact negatively on economic performance.

In contrast, some sociologists and economists argue that the main beneficial economic effects from formal religion involve the social capital formed through interactions with fellow participants. If this social networking effect were the main factor, the impact of higher church attendance on economic growth would be positive, rather than negative, as found in the upper panel of Figure 3.1. Thus, our empirical results suggest that the distinctive feature of formal religion is its promotion of religious beliefs, such as belief in hell.

In most cases, variations across countries or over time in religious participation and beliefs are strongly positively correlated. That is, people who go to church a lot tend also to have high beliefs in hell, heaven, and so on. Therefore, to assess the overall effect of greater religiosity on economic growth, we have to consider a combination of the two effects brought out by Figure 3.1. In this combined effect, greater attendance subtracts from growth, but greater religious belief adds to growth. It turns out that these two effects are similar in size;[11] therefore, the overall connection between religiosity (interpreted as more participation *and* correspondingly more beliefs) and growth is weak. Thus, in most cases, differences in overall religiosity are not the main source of observed differences in economic growth across countries or over time. But the economic effects are important in some cases; as examples, the high religious beliefs in Scandinavian countries and Japan, when compared to their extremely low levels of religious participation, are a spur to economic growth.

Why Religion Matters for Economic Growth

Our central finding is that the effect of religiosity on economic growth involves a positive response to believing *relative* to belonging (attending). We conjecture that religious beliefs stimulate growth because they help to sustain aspects of individual behavior—honesty, thrift, work ethic—that enhance productivity.

Our statistical results do not necessarily imply that greater religious attendance has a net negative influence on economic growth. Rather, the net effect depends on the extent to which an increase in attendance leads to stronger beliefs. That is, the key matter is how effective organized religion is in generating its principal output, which corresponds to the religious beliefs held by its practitioners.

Contrary to the social-capital approach, we find that, for given religious beliefs, greater attendance at formal religious services reduces economic growth. We can think of this effect as a combination of several forces. First, there is a negative effect from the resources used by the religion sector. Second, there may be a positive networking benefit from greater participation in formal religious services because of the increased social interactions. Then, finally, church attendance may be a proxy for the influence of organized religion on a country's laws and regulations. Many of the rules advocated by religions—for example, interferences with credit and insurance markets and with corporate governance, regulations of store hours, and restrictions on individual choices regarding family planning—would be negative for economic activity. We explore this force in detail for Islam in Chapter 4. Our finding is that the overall impact of the various forces associated with greater religious participation, for given religious beliefs, is negative for economic growth.

Protestantism and Human Capital

We already mentioned that Weber ([1904–1905] 1930) suggested that the "Protestant ethic" was a key force favoring economic progress, at least around the time of the Industrial Revolution in Western Europe. Specifically, Weber thought that the ethic of Protestant theology induced followers to work harder and save more.

An alternative—or complementary—view is that Protestantism favors economic growth because it encourages the accumulation of human capital through education. This view relates to Martin Luther's idea that schooling should be used to enable all Christians to read the Bible by themselves, without a priest as intermediary. As stressed by Sascha Becker and Ludger Woessmann (2008), this idea from Luther applied to girls as well as to boys. Then, the resulting high literacy among Protestants would enhance economic development in general, not just reading of the Bible. This idea can be extended to the reading of sacred texts in other religions.

Becker and Woessmann (2009) sought to test the human-capital version of Protestantism's favorable effects on economic growth by using data from Prussia in the late nineteenth century. This place and time provides a natural setting for a study of the relationships among Protestantism, education, and economic prosperity, particularly because the area includes Wittenberg, where Luther began the Protestant Reformation in 1517. (Coincidentally, Prussia was also the birthplace of Max Weber.) Moreover, Prussia had uniform laws and institutions, and its territory included substantial representation of Protestants (Lutherans) and Catholics in the late nineteenth century. Overall, the population was about two-thirds Protestant, one-third Catholic, and 1 percent Jewish.

Figure 3.2 shows the concentration of Protestants in 1871 in Prussian counties, in relation to each county's geographical location relative to Wittenberg (marked by an x). There was substantial variation of Protestant concentration across the counties, ranging from 0 to 100 percent. More than 75 percent of the counties had shares that were at least 80 percent Protestant or less than 20 percent Protestant; that is, many counties were predominantly Protestant or predominantly Catholic.

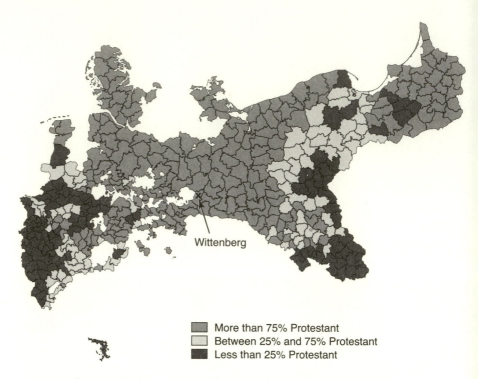

FIGURE 3.2. Protestantism in Prussia, 1871. The pattern shows that Protestants are concentrated in counties close to Wittenberg, the home of Martin Luther. Wittenberg is shown by the x. Becker, Sascha O., and Woessmann, Ludger, "Was Weber Wrong? A Human Capital Theory of Protestant Economic History," *Quarterly Journal of Economics*, 2009, vol. 124, issue 2, by permission of Oxford University Press.

As the figure shows, places close to Wittenberg tended to have much higher concentrations of Protestants in 1871 than those far from Wittenberg. This circular dispersion of Protestant concentration around Wittenberg would not be surprising during the sixteenth century, following Luther's start of the Reformation in 1517. Given the substantial costs of traveling and of information diffusion through space, the closer a county to Luther's home base, the more likely that a princely leader would adopt Luther's innovation and shift an area's main religion from Catholic (the initial situation) to Protestant (Lutheran). Moreover, once these choices were made, the tendency of leaders and families to stick with religion choices suggests that the pattern of Protestantism around Wittenberg could persist many years after the Reformation. It turns out that the forces of persistence are sufficiently strong so that, even after three hundred to four hundred years, being close to Wittenberg still made it much more likely that a county would be heavily Protestant rather than Catholic (as shown in Figure 3.2 for 1871).

A potentially fruitful line of inquiry would be to study the sale of indulgences in principalities radiating out from Wittenberg prior to the Reformation. Wittenberg had banned the sale of the Saint Peter's indulgence sold by Dominican monk Johann Tetzel in 1517 on papal authority. Luther noted how the faithful of Wittenberg, located in Saxony where the sale of the Saint Peter's indulgence had been prohibited, got around the restriction by traveling to nearby Zerbst and Jütterbock in the neighboring principality of Anhalt to purchase the plenary indulgences sold by Tetzel. The two-tiered indulgence economy (local institutions–Vatican) had been changing to a one-tiered system oriented toward the Vatican (Glenn Ehrstine 2018). Data on the sale of indulgences in principalities fanning out from Wittenberg could demonstrate the decline in the indulgence effect on local economies, thereby favoring Protestant entry. On that point, five years after Tetzel appeared in Anhalt, Martin Luther preached in Zerbst.

The Prussian Statistical Office also collected substantial socioeconomic data during the nineteenth century. In particular, the 1871 Prussian Census surveyed the literacy of the whole population. These data cover all 452 of Prussia's then existing counties, and the range of literacy rates across the counties was large, ranging between 37 and 99 percent. Prussia was also exceptional during the nineteenth century in having previously granted freedom of religion to all individuals—Frederick the Great declared around 1740 that all citizens of his country could find salvation in their own way.

Becker and Woessmann (2009) show that predominantly Protestant counties in 1871 had substantially higher literacy rates than predominantly Catholic counties. Going from an all-Catholic place to an all-Protestant one is associated with a rise in the literacy rate by 8 percentage points, compared to an overall average literacy rate of 87.5 percent.

This positive correlation between Protestant concentration and a measure of human capital suggests that Protestantism promoted education even into the nineteenth century. However, there is also the possibility of reverse causation, in particular, Protestants being more attracted than Catholics to places with strong education. This general idea was raised more broadly by R. H. Tawney in criticisms of Weber. For example, in his foreword to Weber's ([1904–1905] 1930) book, Tawney (1930, p. 8) says, "Why insist that causation can work in only one direction? Is it not a little artificial to suggest that capitalist enterprise had to wait, as Weber appears to imply, till religious changes had produced a capitalist spirit? Would it not be equally plausible, and equally one-sided, to argue that the religious changes were themselves merely the result of economic movements?"

To mitigate concerns about reverse causation, Becker and Woessmann focused on the cross-county variation in Protestant concentration that could be explained solely by the distance from Wittenberg, that is, the pattern shown in Figure 3.2. They demonstrated that the effect of Protestantism on literacy is even more powerful in this context—that is, a county being closer to Wittenberg and being more likely for that reason to be heavily Protestant is strongly positively related to literacy.[12]

Becker and Woessmann (2009) went further to relate Protestantism to a measure of per capita income, not just to literacy. The best proxy for per capita county income in nineteenth-century Prussia comes from data on per capita income tax payments in 1877. These tax payments turn out to be significantly positively correlated across the Prussian counties with the share of Protestants in the population. In particular, per capita income tax payments were 9.1 percent higher in 225 mostly Protestant counties than in 102 mostly Catholic counties. Becker and Woessmann show that this positive relationship between Protestantism and their proxy for per capita income holds even when one restricts oneself to the part of Protestant variation that can be explained by a county's distance from Wittenberg.

The bottom line from the Becker and Woessmann (2009) study is that variations in Protestantism across Prussian counties explain substantially higher levels of human capital (in the form of literacy) and per capita income (gauged by income tax payments). This pattern is consistent with Luther's argument that Protestantism provides greater incentives for literacy aimed at individual reading of the Bible. However, this pattern does not rule out additional effects of Protestantism that work through Max Weber's spirit-of-capitalism channel, that is, through the fostering of work ethic and other character traits.

Timo Boppart and colleagues (2013, 2014) applied a Becker-Woessmann-style (2009) analysis to schooling in Switzerland in the late nineteenth century. In the Swiss context, the counterparts to Luther and Wittenberg are the Protestant reformers Huldrych Zwingli and John Calvin and their respective home bases of Zürich and Geneva. Catholics and Protestants were roughly evenly split in Switzerland overall in the late nineteenth century, but, as with Prussia, individual districts tended to be either highly Catholic or highly Protestant. A district's Protestant share of the population was strongly related, inversely, to the distance from Zürich or Geneva (based on which of these two cities was closer to a particular district).

Boppart et al. (2013, Table 4) find that school expenditure per pupil from 1870 to 1888 was negatively related to the Catholic share of a district's population. This pattern accords with Protestantism encouraging investment in formal education.

Boppart et al. (2014) used data by district on outcomes on compulsory standardized tests administered in the late nineteenth century to the male population in various fields, notably reading and mathematics. Hence, their educational data went far beyond the literacy measures available to Becker and Woessmann (2009). Boppart et al. (2014, Tables 3 and 4) find that performance on the reading and math exams was significantly positively related to the Protestant share of a district's population. Moreover, the magnitudes of effects for reading and math were quantitatively similar. For example, shifting from an all-Catholic to an all-Protestant population was found to raise the share of high performers on the reading exam by 18 percentage points and that on the math exam by 19 percentage points. This population change was found to lower the share of failures on the reading exam by 15 percentage points and that on the math exam by 28 percentage points. Hence, these results suggest that Protestantism's favorable impact on education and human capital goes well beyond improvements in basic literacy, which is most plausibly related to reading of the Bible. Instead, the results are consistent with a favorable inclination of Protestantism more broadly to education and human capital.

Finally, Boppart et al. (2014, Tables 5 and 6) find that the positive effects of Protestantism on test outcomes continue to apply when they hold constant measures of school inputs. Hence, they find that Protestantism enhances school productivity in the sense of outcomes achieved per amount invested. A possible explanation for this result is that students and teachers in Protestant environments tended to work harder; that is, the results are consistent with the Protestant work ethic stressed by Weber ([1904–1905] 1930).

To isolate clearly the effects of Protestantism on work ethic, we need data specifically related to this concept. Christoph Basten and Frank Betz (2013) used measures for Switzerland based on voting since 1980 on referenda concerning what they call "preferences for leisure." For example, they had information on referenda on prolonging the length of legally required vacations, lowering the official retirement age, and cutting weekly work hours. They constructed an average indicator of preference for leisure—viewed as the opposite of work ethic—by averaging the votes on the relevant issues. They then compared the vote outcomes for Protestants (the Reformed variants related to Zwingli and Calvin) versus Catholics. To gain convincing identification of the religion effect, they focused on a region in western Switzerland where the current split of the population by religion depended to a large extent on the outcome of long ago wars (in 1476 and 1536). The result of the conflicts was that the present-day cantons of Vaud and Fribourg are exogenously predominantly Protestant and Catholic, respectively. It also turned out that there was a striking shift just at the border between Vaud and Fribourg not only in religious composition but also in political support for the referenda related to preferences for leisure. Basten and Betz (2013, p. 69) concluded from the observed pattern that "Protestant electorate support for increasing leisure time will be about 13.5 percentage points lower than in a Catholic electorate." Hence, there seemed to be a large difference in work ethic, along the lines of Weber's ([1904–1905] 1930) theory.

Jörg Spenkuch (2017) examined the relation of hours worked in contemporary Germany (2000–2008) to individuals' adherence to Protestantism versus Catholicism. To help isolate causation from religion to labor hours, he considered only the variations in recent adherence that could be explained by long-ago religion choices made by princes following the Peace of Augsburg in 1555. His main finding (Table 7) was that Protestants worked a substantial three to four hours more per week than Catholics. However, he found no significant differences between Protestants and Catholics in wages (Table 7) or in years of schooling (Table 9). The lack of an impact on school years likely reflects the broad impact of compulsory schooling laws. Spenkuch's conclusion (p. 212) is that the results "are difficult to reconcile with a human-capital theory of Protestantism. They are consistent, however, with a simple explanation based on values." Hence, this study reinforces that of Basten and Betz (2013) in finding an important difference in work ethic between Protestants and Catholics in the modern period.

Bringing the Two-Way Causation Together

The previous chapter considered causation from economic development to religiousness, and the current one considered causation from religiousness to economy, especially economic growth. We focused on the Weberian view, based on the theologies of Luther, Calvin, and Wesley, that religious beliefs associated with the Protestant Reformation fostered traits such as work ethic and thrift and, thereby, facilitated the Industrial Revolution in the 1700s. In particular, this revolution began earlier in predominantly Protestant countries, such as England, the Netherlands, and parts of Germany, than in Catholic ones, such as France and Italy.

Although Weber did not expect the influence of Protestantism on economic growth to continue through the nineteenth century and beyond, we did find evidence of Weberian effects in the cross-country data since 1960. Specifically, we found that economic growth responded positively to increases in believing (such as in hell and heaven) relative to belonging (gauged by regular attendance at formal religious services). These results suggest that religion matters for economic outcomes primarily as a creator of important beliefs and not so much for its promotion of social interactions.

We assessed the idea, related to Martin Luther's stress on individual reading of the Bible, that Protestantism could influence economic development because of its promotion of education and human capital. The research by Becker and Woessmann (2009) for nineteenth-century Prussia and by Boppart et al. (2013, 2014) for nineteenth-century Switzerland validated this channel of effects. Basten and Betz (2013) and Spenkuch (2017) found direct evidence from modern data for Switzerland and Germany, respectively, that part of religion's effect on economic outcomes involved a positive influence of Protestantism on work ethic.

In terms of future research, it would be good to make further progress in separating religiosity's effects on character traits such as work effort and thrift from those involving education and those involving religion-based laws and regulations. It might work to gauge the character traits by using survey questions from the WVS, which asks, first, how important work is in one's life and, second, whether hard work and thrift should be included in a list of qualities that children can be encouraged to learn at home. These survey data can be linked to individual religious affiliation and to outcomes on education and income. And Jonathan Fox's (2018) *Religion and State* data can be used to assess religion-inspired laws and regulations at the country level.

Islam and Economic Growth

A natural complement to Max Weber's ([1904–1905] 1930) analysis would assess the economic role of beliefs and participation in non-Christian religions. This chapter explores these effects conceptually and empirically for Islam. We discuss toward the end of the chapter analogous research for other world religions, notably Hinduism, Buddhism, and Judaism.

Our discussion of economic growth in Chapter 3 used Weber's insights to explore the role of religiosity as a determinant of economic growth. Weber's analysis focused on the Reformation and the resulting differences between Catholic and Protestant beliefs concerning work ethic, thrift, honesty, accumulation of human capital, and so on. Weber stressed the role of the Protestant ethic at the time of the Industrial Revolution in Western Europe. However, our analysis of modern data isolated a link from beliefs in hell and heaven—interpreted as sticks and carrots for work effort and productivity—to economic growth. More specifically, we found positive effects on growth from high beliefs when compared to levels of participation in formal religious services.

One finding in Chapter 2 is that Muslims stood out in the extent of religious beliefs—particularly high on the existence of hell and heaven. These beliefs were also high when compared to numbers on participation in formal religious services. Given our results about economic growth in Chapter 3, the comparatively high levels of religious beliefs in Muslim countries should have generated high economic growth—a prediction that does not accord with modern data, say since 1960. This pattern might arise because the data on participation in formal religious services understate the time that Muslims typically devote to their religion; much of this time shows up outside of formal services. In addition, there might be adverse effects on economic growth in Muslim countries from religious practices and government regulations. This chapter gives particular weight to the last possibility by considering the economic and political role of Islam over its long history.

By the tenth century, Muslim countries were much more developed and scientifically advanced than European ones. Yet this Muslim economic advantage did not last, and today these countries are much less prosperous than their Western counterparts. The key question is this: what role did religion play in the relative economic decline of Muslim countries?

To set the stage, we can use available data back to 1875 to compare the real per capita GDP of a major Muslim country, Turkey, with that in places—primarily Western European countries and their offshoots—that subsequently formed the OECD (Organisation for Economic Co-operation and Development).[1] The population-weighted average of real per capita GDP for 19 OECD countries in 1875 was $2,690 (in 2000 US dollars), whereas that in Turkey (the central part of the Ottoman Empire at the time) was $1,469; hence, the OECD was 1.8 times richer than Turkey. In a recent year, 2016, the OECD average was $33,273, whereas that in Turkey was $11,649, so that the OECD was 2.9 times richer. So, we can think of using the long-term Muslim history to explain why Turkey was only one-third to one-half as rich as OECD countries in the period from 1875 to 2016.

Muhammad and the Rise of Islam

A confluence of two religious trends in the Arabian Peninsula served as the platform for Muhammad and the rise of Islam.[2] The first was the increasing influence of Christianity, and the second was the significant presence of Jewish communities on the Arabian Peninsula. Polytheism, practiced by Arab tribes in the towns of Mecca and Medina, had coexisted with Abrahamic monotheism and later on Christianity after the Council of Chalcedon in 451. Facing increasing competition from monotheistic religions, polytheism incorporated aspects of monotheism. For example, the god known as Allah, worshipped among a diversity of gods, had taken on the supreme position. Muhammad, who was born in 570, went one step further by insisting that only Allah be worshipped and that he, Muhammad, be recognized as God's prophet. This move on Muhammad's part violated accepted religious practices as well as Meccan tribal political hierarchy.

By creating an exclusive religious-moral legal code for Muslim/ Muslim interaction and a different set of religious-moral rules for Muslim/nonbeliever interaction, particularly when it came to justifying violence toward non-Muslims, the ummah—the Muslim community—became a closed society showing little tolerance toward others. Muhammad's messianic vision for Islam as a community of believers permitted his religious movement to overcome traditional tribal and kinship patterns of loyalty. The role of the traditional tribal council of elders as the decision-making authority was replaced by God and Muhammad, the Prophet of God. Muhammad's community was an innovation among Arab tribes as it forbade warring of any kind against fellow Muslims even if they were of different ethnicities and tribal affiliations. This prohibition further held that Muslim-on-Muslim killing meant that both the perpetrator and the victim went to hell (David Cook, 2007, pp. 45–47).

The concept of martyrdom, central to the success of Islam, highlights the strong motivating nature of beliefs in heaven and hell for

Muslims. Martyrdom encompasses acts such as dying in childbirth or from a venomous snake bite, a disease, or seasickness. A person who says certain ritual prayers and blessings numerous times in difficult circumstances can qualify as a martyr (Cook, 2007, pp. 34–35). The point of going out of one's way to become a martyr was, and remains, to attain a heavenly afterlife (and to avoid hell).

As tribes on the Arabian Peninsula converted to Islam, the pattern of raiding other tribes for booty became obsolete. The expansion of Islam beyond the Arabian Peninsula introduced the practice of tribute on conquered non-Muslims. More importantly, the Qur'an (16:125) states that conversion to Islam can only be through persuasion, not force. In particular, the regime was constrained from engaging in forced conversions among the large numbers of non-Muslims who had been conquered militarily. The need for political stability motivated Muslim leaders to establish institutions that regulated tolerance while restraining conservative Islamic orthodoxy.

Madrasas and Waqfs

Since Muslims were a minority in their conquered territories and could convert non-Muslims only through persuasion, freedom of thought and speech were permitted. Initially, non-Muslims—including Christians, Buddhists, and Jews—were more skilled than their Muslim counterparts in interfaith debates. These challenges motivated Muslims to study logical styles of argumentation, particularly those of Aristotle. Jonathan Israel (2006) and Eric Chaney (2016) suggest that medieval Islam, like the later European Enlightenment, fostered intellectual exchanges, discoveries in the sciences, and a questioning of established ideas and institutions. Although Muslim schools (madrasas) concentrated on Arabic grammar and the basics of Qur'an reading, topics in mathematics, astronomy, logic, and natural sciences were also covered. However, the technical courses were taught for religious purposes, such as calculating inheritances, *zakat*, and time (John L. Berggren 2016). Advanced schooling focused on Qur'anic law and exegesis.

By the middle of the twelfth century, Muslims were becoming the majority in conquered territories, such as the geographic regions we recognize today as Iran, Iraq, Turkey, Syria, and Egypt. Madrasas were established in these regions through royal patronage in the form of a *waqf*, a pious endowment set up by a person for specific purposes (Said Arjomand 1999; Timur Kuran 2004). Viziers and members of the extended royal family established waqfs for madrasas that included stipulations on the content of the curriculum, qualifications for and salaries of faculty and administrators, and infrastructure. Stipulations included the number of students, financial aid, and funds for buildings, hostels, hospitals, and libraries.

As discussed by Kuran (2004), when a benefactor died, his or her waqf was directed by descendants or appointed administrators who continued to ensure the fulfillment of the stipulations. A waqf became associated with a designated social service, such as a road, water supply, madrasa, or mosque. A waqf could, to some extent, substitute for the absence of corporations and for the constraints on inheritance. That is, the creation of a waqf allowed an individual to dedicate the use of his or her resources after death on a perpetual basis. The limitation, however, is that the public-good nature of at least part of a waqf's services limited its appeal to an individual provider and to his or her descendants.

Madrasas became state-sponsored institutions, which appointed religious scholars in various branches of Islamic law, the Qur'an, and Islamic tradition. Two trends materialized during the twelfth century that would change the nature of madrasas. First, often at the behest of a political ruler, madrasas were increasingly used to strengthen the orthodoxy of a particular branch of Islam. Rulers used waqf income to reward their supporters, including religious clerics who frequented their courts and established madrasas. Second, by the thirteenth century, the original stipulations of the waqfs were increasingly overruled by the magistrates of the Shari'a court, often to the benefit of a ruler (Chaney 2013). In Iran, Turkey, and India, the office of the *sadr*, whose function was to ensure the legitimacy

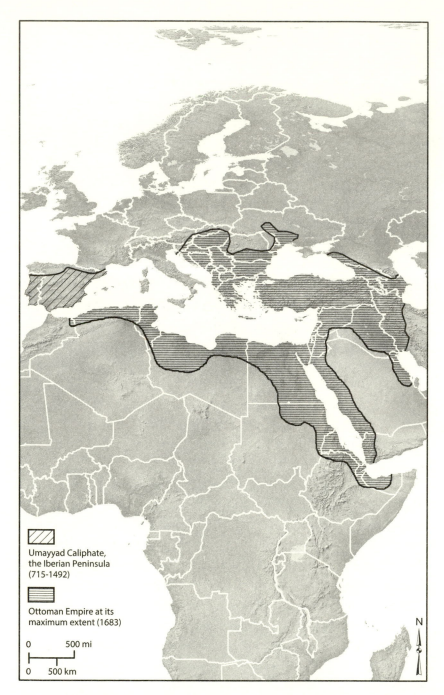

FIGURE 4.1. Map of the Ottoman Empire. Map by C. Scott Walker, Digital Cartography Specialist, Harvard Map Collection.

of the regime and to control the religious sector, administered the waqfs for the madrasas (Arjomand 1999, p. 282). As a consequence, religious elites increasingly served as legitimators of the rulers (Jared Rubin 2017), and madrasas became politicized, losing their original scholarly function.

Decline of Islamic Cultures

Many scholars have observed a "golden age" in scientific and technological production in Muslim countries up to roughly the eleventh century and have pointed to this pattern as evidence that Islam and science are not inherently incompatible. Scientific advances in medicine, mathematics, astronomy, and optics began to be translated into Latin and Greek in the eleventh century (Charles Burnett 2013). In the middle of the twelfth century, the Spanish city of Toledo became the center for translation of texts from Arabic and Greek into Latin. Catholic clerics were intimately involved in the translation of these texts. Popes, the papal curia, archbishops, bishops, and other clerics actively sponsored translations through funding and provision of physical space and the founding of universities where the translations were disseminated and taught.

As the translation work was booming, actual scientific investigation in Muslim countries began to decline from the twelfth century onward. Chaney (2016) documents these patterns of scientific production from data on publications of science books based on entries into Harvard University's library collection. He finds a similar pattern in a catalog of books from seventeenth-century Turkey. He then argues that the likely explanation for the time pattern of scientific production in Muslim countries relates to the growing power of religious elites, combined with the suppression of independent thinking by these elites.

Bernard Lewis (1993) argues similarly that Muslims, rather than being schooled in critical thinking and independent judgment, became occupied with rote learning and memorization. Their principal reliance was on classical texts, with little exposure to new ideas and innovation. Thus, the Islamic world became closed, discouraging reforms by stunting curiosity about the world beyond Islam and deterring intellectual investigation. Islamic scholars contend that, by the twelfth century, Islam had become intellectually rigid, having declared itself perfect without any need of reassessment. All answers had been provided, and all Muslims, to be Muslims, needed only to obey religious authorities.

According to Kuran (1987; 1995, p. iv), preference falsification— whereby people publicly expressed views that deviate from their genuine opinions—became the norm in Muslim societies. Although people may have privately supported social and economic reforms, they abstained from expressing these views publicly and did not attempt to act on them. The motivation for this behavior was to avoid social conflict and punishment (fitna). Thus, an intellectual environment inhospitable to open and honest exchange of ideas for fear of personal retribution came to be the norm.

The static worldview promoted by Islam and found in the ossification of its institutions and policies was buttressed by societal preference falsification. While European societies were engaged into the nineteenth century in social reform, the Islamic world produced no major movements pursuing internal radical social change. And, the reason the Muslim world did not is precisely because its institutions were viewed as stabilizing structures that were indispensable to the political, social, and economic status quo. The ossification of institutions was a symptom of the decline, not the cause.

Kuran (1995) argues that the rise of capitalism in Europe depended on three conditions that were absent in Muslim societies. The first element was the lengthening of chains of action through a growing capacity to control complex networks of production, administration, research, and mass communication. In Western Europe, individualism was valued because it promoted economic growth, not by breaking social ties but by diversifying them and extending them particularly through the use of the legal system.

The second element involved the transformation of legitimate political power from absolute dominance to the rule of law. And a key property of the legal system was its support for economic progress through the allowance for contracts, the enforcement of contract provisions and property rights, and the absence of restrictions on voluntary exchange through credit and insurance and other arrangements. Kuran particularly stresses that corporate contract law—the key to the existence of modern corporations—was a Western European invention.

The third element featured a metamorphosis of religion through the secularization of legal, social, and political institutions. Religion, in Western Europe, was not immune from political and legal reforms as well as social changes. Weber predicted that society would secularize in many dimensions along with economic development. Modernists made the same argument that, if Islamic countries were to develop, they would have to secularize.

Kuran claims that there is truth to this argument. Muslim religious authorities (ulamā) exercised considerable influence over how adherents interpreted their religious beliefs, practices, and values. Scholars point out that the political language of Islam does not contain any precept to rebel against a bad government. Instead, classical Islam obligates citizens to obey a poor ruler.

Kuran finds that clerical resistance to change was not insurmountable. He gives examples of the establishment of Western-style schools in engineering and medicine. However, Kuran's view is that religious aspects of Islam contributed to the economic decline of Muslim countries.

If we go back to the tenth or eleventh century, we find that, consistent with the pattern in output of science books, the Islamic world was broadly more economically advanced than the Western, Christian world. As Kuran (2004, p. 71) put it, "A millennium ago, around roughly the tenth century, the Middle East was an economically advanced region of the world, as measured by standard of living, technology, agricultural productivity, literacy, and institutional creativity. Only China might have been more developed. Subsequently, however, the Middle East failed to match the institutional transformation through which Western Europe vastly increased its capacity to pool resources, coordinate productive activities and conduct exchanges." By the seventeenth century, the Western countries had clearly forged ahead.

While Western European nations were laying the groundwork for the Industrial Revolution particularly in the eighteenth century, Muslim countries were becoming economically stagnant due to an overemphasis on political and social stability. Although this stability was good for economic progress, Islam went too far in supporting the status quo. For example, religious justification was given for market regulations that constrained economic activity. When Europe's economic development began to overtake the Ottoman Empire, the fallback position in the empire was to appeal to religion as a reason not to change. While the West was undergoing a period of growth (increases in income per capita due to technological, institutional, and organizational innovations), the Muslim countries experienced economic stagnation and a decline in scientific and technological investigation. As noted before, by 1875 (our first year of reliable data), the relatively low economic growth in the Ottoman Empire (corresponding to Turkey in our data) showed up as per capita GDP being about half that in the mostly Western European countries that subsequently formed the OECD.

Islamic Law and Regulation

The key to the relative economic decline of Muslim countries especially after the fifteenth century lies in their legal and regulatory institutions.[3] Our analysis of Islamic law and regulation relies particularly on Timur Kuran (2004). He notes that most Islamic legal institutions were not specified in the Qur'an but developed gradually between 661, the end of the reign of Muhammad and his immediate followers, up to around 1000. From then on, crucial aspects of these institutions did not change greatly at least up to the nineteenth century. Moreover, with the Industrial Revolution beginning by the eighteenth century, the restraints implied by Islamic legal structure became an increasing impediment to economic growth.

According to Kuran (2004, p. 74), "Of the few economic rules set forth in the Qur'an, the most detailed and most explicit pertain to inheritance. Two-thirds of any estate is reserved according to intricate rules for a list of extended relatives of both sexes." Thus, inheritance law promoted equality, notably by gender, but also fragmented wealth and discouraged the accumulation of assets. As Kuran (p. 88) notes, "Of the institutions identified here as obstacles to indigenous economic modernization, one that remains largely in place [in the twenty-first century] is the Islamic inheritance system."

With regard to Islamic contract law, a key aspect is its individual nature. Partnerships (not mentioned in the Qur'an) were permitted, but the lives of these entities were compromised by the death of a partner. More specifically, corporations—with a distinct and perpetual legal identity—were not recognized. With no corporate law in the Middle East until 1908, non-Muslims could form corporations, but only under the legal system of a foreign country. They formed corporations headquartered in Paris or London or other European cities as foreign protégés but always as part of a consortia involving foreigners (Kuran 2010, pp. 97–100, 198–202).

Although Muslims were required to use Islamic law in their transactions, Christians and Jews had the option of using Western-style legal arrangements when Muslims were not involved. Kuran argues that this option helps to explain why Christians and Jews tended to outperform Muslims within Muslim countries. The reliance of Muslims on Islamic law became especially burdensome when economies of scale became central for exploiting the technological opportunities offered by the Industrial Revolution.

It is well known that Islamic law constrained the development of credit markets, particularly by limiting interest payments (a restriction possibly contained in the Qur'an). Many mechanisms for evading usury restrictions have been devised and condoned and may have limited the economic impact of these restrictions on credit. However, legal restrictions also applied to insurance contracts, which faced unreliable enforcement by the Islamic legal system.

Kuran (2004, p. 74) argues that Islamic political systems featured insecure property rights, often involving arbitrary impositions of taxes, expropriations of goods, and forced labor provisions, such as for road building. These problems, along with corruption and bribery, may have been more prevalent in Muslim areas than in the West. Starting at least with the Magna Carta in Britain in 1215, the West had some success in limiting central authority and preventing arbitrary taxation.

Muslim Influence on European Conflicts

Murat Iyigun (2008) argues that military campaigns by the Otto-man Empire against Europe had a big impact after the Protestant Reformation on the extent of violent conflicts between Catholics and Protestants within Europe. His idea is that Catholics and Prot-estants were inclined to be allies—or, at least, not fight each other—when they were busy fighting Muslim invaders. Specifically, he finds that military conflicts among Europeans fell by as much as 25 percent when the Muslim threat posed by Suleyman the Magnifi-cent peaked between 1521 and 1566. Muslim victories effectively provided bargaining chips for the budding Protestant movement, whereby alliances against the Ottoman Empire were exchanged for recognition of Lutheranism. This exchange featured prominently in the Peace of Augsburg of 1555, which ushered in a half century of peace among Germany's warring religious factions.

According to Iyigun (2008), the Peace of Augsburg proved to be only a temporary reprieve, because the incentive for peace be-tween Catholics and Protestants weakened along with the decline in the Muslim military threat. Following the great naval defeat of the Ottomans in the Lepanto Sea Battle of 1571, violence between Catholics and Protestants accelerated during the Catholic Counter-Reformation. And the truly murderous sectarian conflict between Protestant reformers and Catholic Counter-Reformers peaked during the Thirty Years' War (1618–1648), whose casualties are es-timated to number between 2.8 and 3.3 million. Iyigun contends that it was no accident that this time of intense religious-based conflict in Europe coincided with military weakness of the Otto-man Empire. It was only with the Peace of Westphalia in 1648 that Catholics and Protestants in Europe reached a state of peaceful coexistence.

The declines of three Muslim empires—Ottomans, Safavids, and Mughals—and the continuing incursions by Western powers led to the colonization of former Islamic territory. Britain eventually controlled India, Burma, Egypt, Palestine, and Jordan. The Nether-lands had Indonesia; France governed Algeria, Lebanon, Syria, and French Morocco; and Spain held Spanish Morocco. After World

War I, the Ottoman Empire was divided into new states, including Turkey, Iraq, Syria, and Saudi Arabia. The small Arab sheikhdoms on the western shore of the Gulf were under British protection until 1971 (in the case of Kuwait, 1961). Although Persia (Iran) was never a colony, Britain competed there with Russia for much of the nineteenth and twentieth centuries.

The Hajj and Ramadan

The five pillars of Islam are, first, belief in Allah as the one true god and in Muhammad as his messenger; second, praying five times per day (dawn, noon, midafternoon, sunset, and nighttime); third, support for the needy (zakat); fourth, fasting during Ramadan; and, fifth, undertaking the Hajj pilgrimage to Mecca at least once in one's lifetime (if one is physically and financially able). Two recent studies by economists concern the last two pillars. First we discuss the Hajj, and next we consider Ramadan.

THE FOSTERING OF RELIGIOUS
TOLERANCE—A STUDY OF THE HAJJ

The Hajj takes place each year in Mecca, Saudi Arabia, starting on the eighth day of the month of Dhu'l Al-Hijjah in the Islamic calendar. The rituals last for five days and, in 2012, were attended by more than three million people from over a hundred countries. Participation in the Hajj has been on the increase for decades, with temporary blips downward in 2013 because of a disease epidemic and in 2014 because of a large construction program in Mecca. In 2012, Hajjis (participants in the Hajj) were about 64 percent male, with 54 percent from outside Saudi Arabia. Hajjis perform identical rituals and dress in similar, simple garments, featuring white sheets for men. This practice promotes a sense of camaraderie and equality, even though participants come from diverse socioeconomic and cultural backgrounds. A study of the Hajj by David Clingingsmith, Asim Khwaja, and Michael Kremer (2009; henceforth CKK) notes that many Hajjis describe the pilgrimage as the most significant religious event in their lives.

From a research standpoint, it is hard to gauge the impact of Hajj attendance on individual behavior and attitudes because the people who come represent what economists call an endogenous selection. For example, people may attend because they are unusually religious or more inclined toward a tolerant global outlook, and so on. To deal with this issue, the CKK study exploited the randomization of attendance offered by available data from the Pakistani lottery of 2006. In that year, out of Pakistan's total quota of 150,000, 90,000 visas were allocated by the government, out of which 89 percent were covered by the lottery. Among the 135,000 who applied for the lottery (in groups of up to 20 persons), 59 percent were successful.[4] Of successful lottery applicants, 99 percent actually attended the Hajj, while only 11 percent of those unsuccessful attended (by paying private tour operators or through special quotas). Thus, the random success in the lottery had great predictive value for whether otherwise similar people attended the Hajj. The CKK study verified that lottery outcomes actually appeared to be random with respect to characteristics such as gender, age, marital status, and education. Therefore, it seems convincing that one can isolate the causal impact of the Hajj by comparing successful with unsuccessful lottery applicants.

The CKK project obtained a list of all Hajj lottery applicants for 2006 from the Pakistani government and then interviewed a selection of these people five to eight months after the Hajj. The survey, covering successful and unsuccessful lottery entrants, is broadly representative of the adult Pakistani population, except that the very rich and very poor tend to be excluded. (The richest tend to use private tour operators, and the poorest tend not to apply at all.)

One finding is that the Hajj raised the tendency to view oneself as religious and substantially increased participation in personal prayer. There was a shift toward Islamic rites that were recognized globally and away from practices more specific to Pakistan.

From the standpoint of tolerance, one finding is that Hajjis were more likely to have formed positive views of persons of many other nationalities, particularly Saudis and Indonesians, who composed the two largest groups in attendance. However, there was no impact on views toward Europeans (who would not have attended the Hajj in significant numbers). There was a general rise in favorable beliefs about Islamic adherents of different sects and ethnicities. However, the Hajj did not change views about the role of religion in politics, including support for political Islam.

Participation in the Hajj made people—men and women—more likely to support an improved status of women along intellectual, spiritual, and moral dimensions. There was enhanced support for education of girls and toward female participation in the labor force. However, the results did not indicate any change in the acceptance of male authority in the household.

The liberalized attitude toward the status of women, to the extent it occurred, may have arisen because women and men, including non–family members, traveled and participated together during the Hajj. As a result, gender mixing was much greater than under normal circumstances in Pakistan. This perspective suggests that the CKK findings might be specific to Pakistan; that is, attitudes toward women may have moved toward the more liberal attitudes prevalent in some other countries, such as Indonesia. Thus, the changes would likely be different for persons coming from countries in which attitudes were already more favorable toward the status of women. To make this comparison, researchers would have to apply the CKK research design to other countries.

RAMADAN AND ECONOMIC GROWTH

Islam stipulates that, with exceptions for age and infirmity, Muslims must refrain from eating or drinking from sunrise to sunset for roughly one month each year, during the period of Ramadan. The period also features an increase in spiritual activities, such as praying and reading the Qur'an. Thus, we can view Ramadan broadly as an expansion of Islamic religious strictness and activity, and we can try to examine how this change impacts outcomes such as the rate of economic growth. From the standpoint of increased fasting and praying, we would predict that Ramadan would lower work effort and productivity and, thereby, retard economic growth.

A study by Filipe Campante and David Yanagizawa-Drott (2015; henceforth CY) emphasizes that, from the scientific perspective of isolating causation from religious strictness to economic outcomes, an attractive feature of Ramadan is that its length varies from one year to the next in a manner dictated by a location's latitude. That is, the variation of the Islamic calendar in relation to the solar calendar—shifting by roughly eleven days each year—means that the number of hours of fasting for each day of Ramadan is longer when Ramadan happens to fall during the summer, and this pattern is accentuated for countries more north of the equator. The opposite pattern holds for winter Ramadans,[5] and the whole configuration is reversed for countries in the southern hemisphere compared to those in the north.

One empirical finding from CY is that, as expected, an expansion of Ramadan hours leads to significantly lower economic growth during the year. Moreover, this effect turns out to be more important the larger the fraction of a country's population that adheres to Islam. At the low end (up to 25 percent adherence), the effects of variations in Ramadan hours on economic growth are essentially zero. This pattern makes sense because changes in these hours should matter directly only for the Muslim population. The conformity of the data with this sensible idea makes it more persuasive that CY's results are actually isolating economic effects from changes in Ramadan hours.

As a quantitative example, the CY study compares two predominantly Muslim countries, Bangladesh and Turkey, where the former is much closer to the equator. Therefore, in a year with a summer Ramadan, Turkey has an increase in Ramadan hours compared to Bangladesh, and the consequence is that Turkey grows slower compared to Bangladesh by a sizable one percentage point per year. In years with winter Ramadans, the effects are reversed, and Turkey tends to grow faster compared to Bangladesh by about one percentage point per year. Since the growth effects reverse over time, the impact of Ramadan on the level of per capita GDP is temporary—not a permanent influence on the relative levels of per capita GDP of Turkey and Bangladesh.

Even though the effects are only temporary, the estimated impact on economic growth—by one percentage point per year in the above example—is quantitatively meaningful when compared to other determinants of economic growth that researchers have been able to isolate. Thus, the results suggest more broadly that variations in the extent of religiosity can matter significantly for economic outcomes. These findings are consistent with the growth effects from religious participation and beliefs that we discussed in Chapter 3.

Campante and Yanagizawa-Drott (2015) also studied the influence of variation in Ramadan hours on subjective well-being, gauged by answers to questions about happiness in the World Values Survey. Interestingly, CY found that longer Ramadan hours increase subjective well-being, even though they retard economic growth. A reasonable explanation is that, for the typical Muslim, the enjoyment and spiritual benefits from a longer Ramadan are worth the cost in terms of foregone economic goods.

Other Religions

Many studies in the economics of religion have been inspired by Max Weber's idea of the Protestant ethic and have, therefore, focused on the economic implications of alternative forms of Christianity. However, there are parallel issues in the other main international religions, as explored by Rachel McCleary (2007) in terms of the nature of salvation and on how individual action influences a person's chances of salvation. This chapter has emphasized economic implications of Islam. Now we sketch findings pertaining to other major religions.

HINDUISM AND BUDDHISM

Although Hinduism does not have heaven and hell in the Judeo-Christian sense, one can think of salvation as corresponding to knowledge of ultimate reality, a state of liberation from worldly concerns. The accompanying enlightenment is obtained gradually through reincarnation, as one works toward perfection in successive physical bodies. The belief in reincarnation relates to karma, which is linked to past acts and circumstances, such as caste, that are beyond a person's control at the present time. However, people do possess a free will that allows them to undo past wrongs with morally corrective actions. In this view, individuals are responsible for their ultimate salvation or damnation through their own moral behavior: "Bad karma is the result of (1) failing to perform obligatory acts ... of one's caste and stage of life, (2) performing a prohibited act or (3) being attached to sensual pleasures" (McCleary 2007, p. 54). From the perspective of economic incentives, it is significant that Hinduism views the righteous acquisition of wealth as praiseworthy, as it is needed to fulfill one's duties to family and society.

Sriya Iyer (2018, chap. 2) notes that Hinduism features multiple gods, without a stress on one main scripture or deity. Attendance at formal religious services is deemphasized, when compared to Christianity. In the Hindu religion, conduct is more important than a set of religious beliefs. Emphasis applies to carrying out one's obligations, some of which involve the caste system, which is a regime that restricts mobility and change. These features, combined with the fatalism that attaches to aspects of karma, led to the notion of a "Hindu rate of growth," which connotes a system in which people and governments are supposedly satisfied with mediocre economic performance. However, Dani Rodrik and Arvind Subramanian (2005) counter this idea by arguing that the shift in India in the late 1980s away from economic stagnation and toward persistently high growth was caused by an "attitudinal shift" of the government toward a pro-business—and, we would say, pro-market—stance. Implicitly, they are saying that the shift in India toward policies that promote economic growth was not caused by a change in Hindu economic perspectives.

As discussed in McCleary (2007), Buddhism arose out of Hinduism in India some five hundred years before Christ and gradually became prominent in parts of East Asia. While featuring many doctrinal aspects of Hinduism, including reincarnation, Buddhism emphasizes meditation and contemplation as instruments of gaining salvation (nirvana). There is a stress on the middle way, which features neither extreme asceticism nor extreme sensuality. And Buddhism puts more weight than Hinduism on charity, particularly when directed to family and friends and the community of monks. As with Hinduism, Buddhism values justly acquired wealth because it enables the carrying out of obligations. In Chapter 6, we consider Buddhism in the context of the political and economic forces that underlay the creation of a Buddhist state religion in Tibet.

JUDAISM

A good deal of research has considered the economic implications of Judaism. Maristella Botticini and Zvi Eckstein (2012) try to explain why Jews became highly educated and specialized in fields such as medicine, trade, and financial services, including the provision of credit. They note that a standard argument emphasizes persistent discrimination against Jews along with the portability of human capital, which is harder than physical assets to expropriate. Religious prohibitions against types of economic activity, for example, usury in Christianity and Islam, created the demand for a financial intermediary, thereby leading to occupational specialization among Jews in financial matters, particularly as providers of credit (Irena Grosfeld et al. 2013).

The idea is that an economic prohibition, such as on usury, practiced and enforced by a majority religion, leads to occupational specialization for minorities who are not subject to the prohibition. Resentment against Jewish moneylenders then naturally arose, argue Grosfeld and colleagues (2013). Nico Voigtländer and Hans-Joachim Voth (2012) and Grosfeld et al. (2013) show that the anti-Semitic and anti-market beliefs and attitudes continued to be held and practiced by the majority population even when the minority Jewish population was no longer present.

Botticini and Eckstein (2012) study Judaism's emphasis on individual reading of sacred texts, including the Torah, leading thereby to widespread literacy. In their view, high human capital, not religious persecution and the portability of human capital, is the main explanation for Jewish dominance of fields such as moneylending, medicine, commerce, and trade and for the high levels of international migration. Jews had a comparative advantage in fields that required literacy or numeracy, thereby leading them to concentrate in occupations such as merchant, trader, and moneylender. The Botticini-Eckstein argument parallels that of Becker and Woessmann (2009), who focused on Luther's advocacy of individual reading of the Bible and the resulting increase in Protestant literacy compared to that for Catholics.

One surprise is that Botticini and Eckstein (2012) say almost nothing about Jewish religious beliefs as a driver of economic outcomes. There is no parallel to Weber's ([1904–1905] 1930) Protestant ethic and its connection to hard work, thrift, and honesty. There is also nothing about Jewish beliefs concerning salvation, including the presence or absence of an afterlife, the reality of heaven and hell, and so on. What is clear is that the pursuit of salvation is not a central element in Judaism.

Other scholars confirm that it was Jewish human capital and market presence, not religious beliefs, that stimulated economic growth in Europe prior to the Industrial Revolution (Noel D. Johnson and Mark Koyama 2017). In preindustrial Europe, cities where Jewish communities were allowed to foster benefited from improved market access, thereby experiencing higher economic growth than in cities that banned Jews. Through extensive and well-integrated networks of merchants and financiers reaching as far as the Americas, Jews created a robust network of commerce and trade. The expansion of markets and trade by Jewish networks helped to stimulate economic growth that spread throughout Europe.

Islam and Other World Religions

Chapter 3 assessed effects of religiousness on economic growth, and this chapter has applied that form of analysis specifically to Islam. Muslim countries were leaders in scientific discovery up to the eleventh century and were relatively economically advanced up to the sixteenth and seventeenth centuries. In the early period, Muslim success related to openness to intellectual inquiry and debate,

particularly in places that had previously been conquered militarily. However, by the eleventh century, Muslim societies had shifted
to being more closed and to a focus on stability rather than the creation of new ideas and technical advances. Scientific output, measured by production of books, decreased from the eleventh century
onward.

Islamic legal and regulatory institutions were particularly ill
suited to the economic opportunities offered by the Industrial
Revolution starting at least by the eighteenth century. Problematic
areas included rigid inheritance laws that prevented long-term
wealth accumulation, weak contract enforcement, restrictions on
credit and insurance, and the lack of a legal basis for corporate
structure. These restrictions compromised the ability of companies
to exploit the economies of scale in new forms of manufacturing
and were, therefore, especially constraining during the Industrial
Revolution.

Western expansion of Muslim rule into the West peaked by the
late 1500s. The military conflicts with European powers in the 1500s
and 1600s featured a connection with fighting between Catholics
and Protestants. When Muslim forces were threatening, Catholics and
Protestants tended to unite against a common enemy. But, once
the Muslim challenge had ebbed by the late 1500s, Catholics and
Protestants were more inclined to fight each other, eventually leading to sustained warfare during the Thirty Years' War of 1618–1648.
This religious-based conflict ended only with the Peace of Westphalia in 1648.

Two of the five pillars of Islam are participation in the Hajj (annual pilgrimage to Mecca) and fasting during the month of Ramadan. A study of Hajj participants from Pakistan found that this experience heightened religiosity and expanded tolerance toward
people from other countries. Hajjis tended to become more liberal
with regard to the role of women in society, including having women
attain education and gain better access to labor markets. However,
this liberality did not change views on the role of men as leaders
of households or on the role of religion in politics and the law. An
important question is this: how might the heightened feelings of

tolerance (or Muslim oneness) help resolve regional conflicts between Sunni and Shia Muslims?

Unlike the Hajj, Ramadan is a family religious holiday practiced in one's home, neighborhood, and mosque. Ramadan entails fasting daily, from sunrise to sunset, for an entire month. One study found that Ramadan reduces economic activity, gauged by per capita GDP. However, the fluctuations in per capita GDP were accompanied by movements in the opposite direction in indicators of happiness. The fasting's adverse physiological and psychological effects on productivity and the spending of time on Ramadan activities diminished production but made people happier—people thought it worthwhile to give up material goods for the satisfaction gained from practicing Ramadan.

Many questions are unanswered by this study of Ramadan. Does Ramadan reinforce strong ties across the Muslim faith as does the Hajj? Or are the effects of Ramadan local, solidifying kinship and communal relationships? What effect does Ramadan have on participants' attitudes toward non-Muslims and others who do not fast during working hours? Does Ramadan create resentment toward non-fasting colleagues?

Research on economic implications of religion has traditionally emphasized Christianity—notably Max Weber's distinction between Protestantism and Catholicism—and Islam—especially the effects from Islamic laws and regulations. Future work could usefully be applied to other world religions, including variations within a broad religion, for example, varieties of Islam. We touched briefly on analyses of Hinduism, Buddhism, and Judaism, but this work could be substantially expanded. And there are many other interesting cases, including the economic role of Confucianism—if that system of philosophy and ethics that originated in China is viewed as a religion.

5

State Religion

Our analysis in previous chapters brought out economic and social effects from government regulation of the religion market and from the government's favoring an official or state religion. In Chapter 2, we found that the subsidies associated with state religions could induce greater religious participation but that government regulation of the religion market tended to suppress this participation. In Chapter 3, we used these relationships to help isolate effects from religiosity on economic growth. In Chapter 4, we argued that economic development was held back by the inclination of Muslim countries beginning in the eleventh century to regulate economic activity so as to conform with Islamic law and theology.

Despite the potential negative consequences, governments tend to establish state religions or otherwise regulate the religion market. These practices often go back hundreds of years. Using a concept of state religion employed in our research (Barro and McCleary 2005) and detailed below, we found for 188 countries that 40 percent had a state religion in 2000, whereas 59 percent had one in 1900. According to the Pew Research Center (2017b), the 40 percent number for state religion still applied in 2017. In 2000, among the seventy-five state religions that we observed, twenty-nine were Islamic, twenty-two were Catholic, ten were Protestant, eight were Orthodox, four were Buddhist, one was Hindu, and one was Jewish.

Islamic state religions were common in 2000 among predominantly Muslim countries, especially in the Middle East and North Africa. Many Latin American and a few European countries still had Catholic state religions, whereas a Protestant state religion still prevailed in England and most of Scandinavia. Most American colonies started with official religions, but a central part of the US Constitution ruled out the establishment of a state religion at the national level. In the present chapter, we seek to understand these choices. Which countries have state religions? And why?

We mentioned in Chapter 2 that Adam Smith's (1791) perspective on state religion, influenced by the Anglican state church in England, underlies the religion-market model developed by the sociologists Rodney Stark and Roger Finke and the economist Laurence Iannaccone. Their argument was that a state religion amounts to a government-sponsored monopoly of the religion sector. The result is poor "service," leading to a decline in religious participation and beliefs. In contrast, the competition and diversity provided by upstart religions, such as Methodism in England and pentecostalism in Latin America, create a healthy environment with enthusiastic participation. Long ago, Alexis de Tocqueville ([1835] 2000) in *Democracy in America* noted the diversity of US religious offerings and argued that this rich array of choices underlay the high levels of church attendance and religious beliefs.

This Smithean-style analysis takes as given the presence or absence of a state religion. But why is it that some countries at some dates had a state religion whereas others did not? To address this question, we view state religion as an institutional/political choice that we analyze through social-science methodology. That is, we take as the dependent variable—the one that we seek to explain based on other variables—the political choice of an institution, namely the presence or absence of a state religion. More specifically, our approach views this choice as corresponding to an institution that is optimal in some sense, given the characteristics of a country. However, because there are large costs to a society from changing institutions, the prevailing regime—here the presence or absence of a state religion—may deviate for a long time from its long-run target value.

Our approach fits with the inclination of economists and other social scientists to apply their methodologies to a wide array of important social issues. Although this tendency is sometimes characterized as imperialistic, it can nevertheless be useful. For example, political economy has been fruitfully applied to understand the degree of democracy, the extent of official corruption and maintenance of the rule of law, and other institutional features. In the same spirit, we analyze why and when a state religion exists. Anthony Gill (2005) provides a complementary analysis of why governments choose whether to regulate the religion market or to promote religious liberty. He stresses the roles of competition among political rivals and the extent to which government regulation of the religion market is adverse for economic outcomes.

The status of state religion matters because it can potentially affect outcomes such as the frequency of church attendance and the strength of religious beliefs (as in Chapter 2). State religion may also be important because it ultimately influences macroeconomic outcomes, such as the rate of economic growth (as discussed in Chapter 3).

Another reason why a study of the choice of state religion is interesting for economists and political scientists is that, over the past two thousand years, state monopoly over religion has been one of the most important forms of politically supported monopoly in existence.[1] Thus, decisions about state religions may tell us something more general about why governments choose to promote monopoly in some sectors but not in others.

Many state religions go back hundreds of years and were introduced for reasons unrelated to forces that operated in the twentieth and twenty-first centuries. For example, the Protestant Reformation initiated in Germany and Switzerland by Martin Luther, John Calvin, and Ulrich Zwingli in the early 1500s partly shapes today's status of organized religion in many countries. Historically, political leaders have been more important than theological ones in influencing the institutionalization of religion. For England, the current Anglican environment reflects Henry VIII's ouster of the Catholic Church in 1534, purportedly over the pope's refusal to grant permission for a divorce, but probably more related to Henry VIII's intention of asserting his royal authority over Catholic institutions and abolishing any competition by confiscating all church property and destroying relics (Bernard 2011). Similarly, the long-lasting presence of the Lutheran state church in Sweden (until 2000) and elsewhere in Scandinavia stems from the ouster of the Catholic Church in 1527 by the Swedish King Gustav Vasa, also motivated by the taking of church property (in this case, to finance military conflicts).

Our analysis does not attempt to explain the motivations of Henry VIII in 1534 or Gustav Vasa in 1527. Going back further, we do not explain why the Orthodox Church separated from the Roman Catholic Church in the Great Schism of 1054, why Christianity and Islam became the state religions of many countries much earlier, or why Buddhism arose out of Hinduism in India some five hundred years before Christ and gradually became prominent in parts of East Asia. Operationally, our empirical research (detailed in Barro and McCleary 2005) takes as given the status of state religion in a region at some point in the past, and for us, the relevant date is a relatively recent one, 1900. This year is the earliest time at which we have a broad classification of countries in terms of the status of state religion.

Studying State Religion

Our study categorizes state religion as an all-or-nothing choice and focuses on three dates at which we have good data: 2000, 1970, and 1900. Our classifications came primarily from the work of David Barrett and his team.[2] This source provides global coverage on a reasonably consistent basis going back to 1900. Although the designations are influenced by legal provisions, including statements about religion in constitutions, the concept employed is ultimately de facto; that is, it is guided by actual practice with respect to the government's favoring the chosen religion or constraining alternative religions. The classifications are clearer in some cases than others. In many situations, the constitution designates an official state religion and restricts or prohibits other forms. However, even without these provisions, governments sometimes favor a designated religion through subsidies and tax collections or through the mandatory teaching of forms of religion in public schools. These considerations caused us to classify some countries as having a "state religion" despite the absence of an official state religion in the constitution. Controversial cases of this type in 2000 include Italy, Portugal, and Spain, which were deemed by Barrett (and us) to have a Catholic state religion at that date.[3]

It is worthwhile to introduce British sociologist David Martin's (1978) classification of religion vis-à-vis the state.[4] Consistent with Barrett, Martin classifies Italy, Portugal, and Spain as the most monopolistic Catholic societies in the world. On a continuum running from Catholic/monopoly at one end to Protestant/pluralism at the other, Martin describes the United States as the most pluralistic society with respect to religion. In between the two extremes are varieties of "mixed" patterns of religion-society relations, among them a category Martin calls "duopoly," referring to large-scale rival monopolies such as those between Catholicism and Protestantism in the Netherlands, Germany, and Switzerland. Two findings related to Martin's classifications are that (1) a Catholic monopoly will give rise to militant opposition usually in the form of secularization and (2) a Protestant majority or a country with a Protestant heritage will generate democratic forms of governance.

Our study covers 188 countries that were independent in 2000. The fractions having a state religion were 40 percent (75 countries) in 2000, 39 percent (73 countries) in 1970, and 59 percent (111 countries) in 1900.[5] Thus, the data for the twentieth century indicate a downward trend in state religion in the first part of the century but no trend from 1970 to 2000.[6]

Figures 5.1 and 5.2 show the worldwide patterns in state religion in 1900 and 2000. The details for selected countries (omitting most small countries) in 1900, 1970, and 2000 are in Table 5.1.

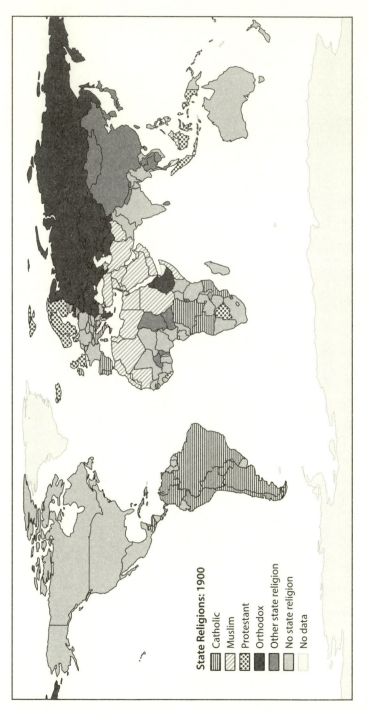

FIGURE 5.1. State religions in 1900. Map by Jeff Blossom, Center for Geographic Analysis, Harvard University.

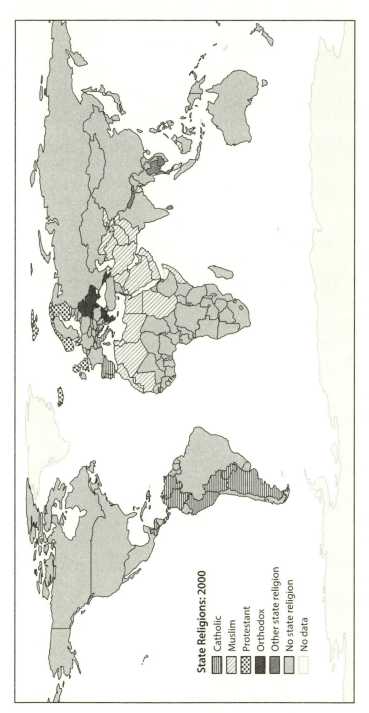

State Religions: 2000

- Catholic
- Muslim
- Protestant
- Orthodox
- Other state religion
- No state religion
- No data

FIGURE 5.2. State religions in 2000. Map by Jeff Blossom, Center for Geographic Analysis, Harvard University.

In terms of transitions, the 188 countries break down into three main groups. The first group, 72 countries, maintained no form of state religion throughout our sample, in 1900, 1970, and 2000. Examples are Australia, Canada, France, Germany, India, Mexico, and the United States.

France in 1900 is ambiguous because it moved gradually away from a Catholic state religion under the Third Republic, a secularization process that started in 1871. The term *laïcité* came into use during this period to denote a national educational program devoid of clerics and Catholic teaching (Charles Glenn 2017, pp. 68–69). In 1903, the French government expelled approximately twenty thousand members of religious orders from the country. In the following year, a law passed that prohibited any member of a religious community from teaching in the schools. This process of secularization (the *laïcisime* of France) culminated in 1905 with a law that proclaimed the independence of church and state. Hence, France clearly had no established state religion as of 1905.

The US case is interesting because most of the original colonies had forms of state religion before the American Revolution. The Anglican Church was the official religion (in the form of the Episcopal Church) of the largest number of colonies, notably in the South. The Congregationalist Church (related to Presbyterianism) dominated in New England, except for Rhode Island, which maintained separation between church and state. The Congregationalist Church was not disestablished until 1818 in Connecticut, 1819 in New Hampshire, and 1824 and 1833—in two phases—in Massachusetts. The US constitutional prohibition against establishment of an official religion, a part of the Bill of Rights, was not applied to state governments until the extension of the Equal Protection Clause of the Fourteenth Amendment to state governments starting in the late 1800s. This extension culminated in a Supreme Court decision in 1934.[7]

Germany is an example of a country that has subsidized more than one organized religion (in this case, Catholicism and Protestantism mainly in the form of Lutheranism) but did not choose a single state religion. We classified Germany as lacking a state religion. Mexico is an example of a Latin American country that once had a Catholic state religion derived from Spanish colonial rule but moved after independence (in 1821) toward separation of church and state. In Mexico, the legally favored status of the Catholic Church ended by 1857.

India's population is three-quarters Hindu, but because the country is so large, the numbers of minority religionists are also large. In 2000, the number Muslim was over 120 million and the number Christian was over 60 million. Perhaps these large numbers of many forms of religious adherence are what Mark Twain was referring to when he quipped during his trip to India and Sri Lanka in 1896, "In religion, all other countries are paupers. India is the only millionaire." Probably because of the large numbers of non-Hindus, India has not maintained a state religion since its independence from Britain in 1948.

A second group, with fifty-eight countries, had a state religion at all three sample dates: 1900, 1970, and 2000.[8] Each of these countries maintained only one type of state religion at the three dates: twenty-one had Catholic state religions, twenty-two had Islam, nine had Protestant (including Anglican), one (Greece) had Orthodox, four had Buddhist, and one (Nepal) had Hindu.

The twenty-one countries with persistent Catholic state religions are in Latin America (thirteen) or Western Europe (eight). As mentioned before, the classifications of some of the European cases—especially Italy, Portugal, and Spain—as having state religions even in 2000 are controversial because the governments have moved during the twentieth century away from the legally favored status of the Catholic Church.

The twenty-two countries with persistent Islamic state religions reflect the striking pattern whereby most countries with predominantly Muslim populations feature governments that favor Islam and restrict other organized religions. Two noteworthy outliers among predominantly Muslim countries are Turkey, which established a democratic regime with separation of church and state under President Mustafa Kemal Atatürk in 1923, and Syria, which moved with its 1973 constitution under the dictator Hafez al-Assad toward a secular regime. These cases show that the lack of state religion in a predominantly Muslim country is not a good indicator of democracy.

Notable among the nine countries with persistent Protestant state religions is England, which has had an Anglican state religion since Henry VIII's separation from the Catholic Church in 1534. Four Scandinavian countries—Denmark, Finland, Iceland, and Norway —maintained Lutheranism as the state religion since the expulsion of the Catholic Church by the Swedish King Gustav Vasa in 1527. (Sweden dropped its state religion in 2000.)

Thailand and Cambodia are predominantly Buddhist countries. They have each maintained Buddhist state religions, except during the period of communist rule (1975–1989) in Cambodia.

A third group of countries, also numbering fifty-eight, had some kind of transition for state religion between 1900 and 2000. Forty-one of these countries had state religions in 1900, subsequently abandoned state religion, and did not reinstitute state religion by 2000. Examples are Brazil, Chile, and Ireland (which dropped the Catholic state church), Syria and Turkey (Islam), Indonesia (which dropped the Dutch Reformed Church imposed by the former colonial ruler), Russia (Orthodox), Sweden (Protestant), Japan (Shinto), and China and Korea (Confucianism).

The dropping of the Orthodox state church with the Russian Revolution in 1918 illustrates a general pattern whereby communist countries lack state religions (with the exception of Somalia in the 1970s). For China, we treated Confucianism as the state religion in 1900; however, this treatment is controversial because Confucianism is often viewed more as a philosophy or system of social ethics rather than as a formal religion. In any event, China clearly lacked a state religion during the post-1948 communist period.

The elimination of the Lutheran state church in Sweden in 2000 is notable because this institution had been in place since 1527. However, this state-supported religion had coexisted for many years with freedom of religion. Other Scandinavian countries—Denmark, Finland, Iceland, and Norway—have continued beyond 2000 with their Protestant state religions, while also maintaining religious freedom. This pattern shows that an official state religion does not necessarily mean that religious liberties are absent or that entry into the religious market is heavily restricted.

A group of twelve countries had a state religion in 1900, dropped the state religion by 1970, but then reinstituted a state religion by 2000. These cases are all former republics of the Soviet Union or Yugoslavia, and the lack of a state religion in 1970 reflected the presence of a communist government. Four Asian countries that were previously parts of the Soviet Union had Orthodox state religions in 1900 but adopted Islamic state religions by 2000.[9] In these cases, the new form of state religion (Islam) conformed with the dominant religious affiliation of the population, rather than the preferences of the Russian emperor (Orthodox). Six other former Soviet or Yugoslav republics, including Armenia and Ukraine, reinstated an Orthodox state religion by 2000. By 2000, Azerbaijan went back to an Islamic state religion, and Croatia returned to a Catholic state religion.

A final group of five countries had no state religion in 1900 but introduced one by 2000. Three of these countries were not independent entities in 1900. Israel adopted a Jewish state religion with its independence in 1948; Pakistan instituted an Islamic state religion in 1956, a few years after its separation from India; and Bangladesh adopted an Islamic state religion in 1975, soon after its separation from Pakistan (following a short interval, 1972–1975, of no state religion). Bulgaria instituted an Orthodox state religion in 2001. We classified Bulgaria as lacking a state religion in 1900, but this classification is ambiguous because it was then subject to competing influences from the Russian (Orthodox) and Ottoman (Islamic) empires. The final case is Vanuatu, a small island that introduced a Protestant state religion upon independence in 1979.

Determinants of State Religion

We carried out a formal statistical analysis of the presence or absence of state religion for 188 countries observed in 1900, 1970, and 2000. We interpret the results as providing information about how

TABLE 5.1. International Patterns of State Religion for Selected Countries, 1900–2000

Country	1900	1970	2000
Afghanistan	Muslim	Muslim	Muslim
Algeria	Muslim	Muslim	Muslim
Argentina	Catholic	Catholic	Catholic
Armenia	Orthodox	none	Orthodox
Australia	none	none	none
Azerbaijan	Muslim	none	Muslim
Bangladesh	none	Muslim	Muslim
Belarus	Orthodox	none	Orthodox
Belgium	none	none	none
Bolivia	Catholic	Catholic	Catholic
Botswana	Protestant	none	none
Brazil	Catholic	none	none
Bulgaria	none	none	Orthodox
Cambodia	Buddhist	Buddhist	Buddhist
Canada	none	none	none
Chile	Catholic	none	none
China	Confucian	none	none
Colombia	Catholic	Catholic	Catholic
Costa Rica	Catholic	Catholic	Catholic
Croatia	Catholic	none	Catholic
Cuba	Catholic	none	none
Denmark	Protestant	Protestant	Protestant
Egypt	Muslim	Muslim	Muslim
Ethiopia	Orthodox	Orthodox	none
Finland	Protestant	Protestant	Protestant
France	none	none	none
Germany	none	none	none
Greece	Orthodox	Orthodox	Orthodox
Guatemala	Catholic	Catholic	Catholic
Hungary	none	none	none
India	none	none	none
Indonesia	Protestant	none	none
Iran	Muslim	Muslim	Muslim
Iraq	Muslim	Muslim	Muslim
Ireland	Catholic	Catholic	none
Israel	none	Jewish	Jewish
Italy	Catholic	Catholic	Catholic
Japan	Shinto	none	none
Jordan	Muslim	Muslim	Muslim
Kazakhstan	Orthodox	none	none
Korea (South)	Confucian	none	none
Kyrgyz Republic	Orthodox	none	Muslim
Laos	Buddhist	Buddhist	none
Liberia	Protestant	Protestant	Protestant
Lithuania	Catholic	none	none

TABLE 5.1. (*continued*)

Country	1900	1970	2000
Malaysia	Muslim	Muslim	Muslim
Mexico	none	none	none
Mongolia	Buddhist	none	none
Morocco	Muslim	Muslim	Muslim
Nepal	Hindu	Hindu	Hindu
Netherlands	none	none	none
Nicaragua	none	none	none
Nigeria	none	none	none
Norway	Protestant	Protestant	Protestant
Pakistan	none	Muslim	Muslim
Peru	Catholic	Catholic	Catholic
Philippines	none	none	none
Poland	none	none	none
Portugal	Catholic	Catholic	Catholic
Romania	Orthodox	none	none
Russia	Orthodox	none	none
Saudi Arabia	Muslim	Muslim	Muslim
Singapore	none	none	none
Slovenia	Catholic	none	none
Somalia	Muslim	Muslim	Muslim
South Africa	none	none	none
Spain	Catholic	Catholic	Catholic
Sri Lanka	Buddhist	Buddhist	Buddhist
Sudan	Muslim	Muslim	Muslim
Sweden	Protestant	Protestant	none
Switzerland	none	none	none
Syria	Muslim	Muslim	none
Tajikistan	Orthodox	none	Muslim
Thailand	Buddhist	Buddhist	Buddhist
Tunisia	Muslim	Muslim	Muslim
Turkey	Muslim	none	none
Turkmenistan	Orthodox	none	Muslim
Ukraine	Orthodox	none	Orthodox
United Kingdom	Protestant	Protestant	Protestant
United States	none	none	none
Uruguay	none	none	none
Uzbekistan	Orthodox	none	Muslim
Venezuela	Catholic	Catholic	Catholic
Vietnam	none	none	none

Year	1900	1970	2000
Total observations	188	189	188
No state religion total	77	116	113
Buddhist (incl. Shinto)	7	5	4
Catholic	35	27	22

Continued on next page

TABLE 5.1. (*continued*)

Year	1900	1970	2000
Confucian	4	0	0
Ethno-religion	7	0	0
Hindu	1	1	1
Islam	31	25	29
Jewish	0	1	1
Orthodox	13	3	8
Protestant	13	11	10

Note: The countries enumerated do not include many with very low populations. Numbers shown by types of religions and groups are for all countries, including those not described individually. Summary of types for 1900, 1970, and 2000: Group 1: no state religion throughout, 72. Group 2: state religion throughout, 58. Group 3: dropped state religion by 1970 and no reinstatement, 29. Group 4: dropped state religion between 1970 and 2000 and no reinstatement, 12. Group 5: dropped state religion by 1970, reinstated by 2000, 12. Group 6: first introduced state religion by 1970 and then retained, 3. Group 7: first introduced state religion between 1970 and 2000 and then retained, 2.

Barro, Robert J., and McCleary, Rachel M. "Which Countries Have State Religions?" *Quarterly Journal of Economics*, 2005, vol. 120, issue 4, pp. 1336–1339, by permission of Oxford University Press.

country characteristics influence the probability that a state religion exists at a particular point in time.

One powerful but unsurprising empirical finding is that the presence of state religion is strongly positively related to the concentration of persons in a country's most popular religion. Countries where almost all people are Islamic or Catholic are particularly likely to have an Islamic or Catholic state religion. Moreover, this linkage does not depend a lot on which type of religion is the main one. The one exception is a positive effect on the probability of having a state religion when the dominant religion is Islam. There are only a few countries with close to 100 percent Islamic adherence that do not have a state religion (including Syria and Turkey at recent times).

Given the fraction of persons who adhere to the main religion, the fraction that adhere to the second most popular religion turns out not to matter for the probability of state religion. Our conjecture had been that concentration into this second group—as contrasted with dispersion across many minority religions—would have made state religion less likely. However, the data do not support that hypothesis.

Our analysis classified religious adherence from the perspective of a standard grouping of religions: Catholic, Mainline Protestant (including Anglican), other Protestant (mainly evangelicals of various types), Orthodox, Jewish, Islam, Hindu, Buddhist, other Eastern religions, other religions, and no religion. One question about this division is whether the pressure for state religion depends on the total concentration within one of our groups or on the division among types—for example, Sunnis versus Shias within the Islam category. Similarly, is it the total number of Christians that influences the maintenance of a state religion, or is the division among subtypes (Catholic, Mainline Protestant, other Protestant, and Orthodox) important?

The results for predominantly Muslim countries provide a clear answer: state religion relates to the total mass of Muslims, with the division into types being secondary. As an example, a state religion was implemented in Iraq with its new constitution in 2005, even though the country featured substantial representation across Shias and Sunnis and other types. Article 2 states unambiguously, "Islam is the official religion of the State and is a foundation source of legislation.... No law may be enacted that contradicts the established provisions of Islam."

Another interesting case is Turkey, which, as part of the Ottoman Empire, historically had an Islamic state religion. Following the collapse of the empire after World War I, the former military leader and subsequently President Atatürk established a secular republic, which has been in place since 1923. However, although Atatürk in 1924 abolished the Ottoman Caliphate, which had been in existence since 1517, Turkey has never really separated religion from the state. In fact, the state controls religion through its Directorate of Religious Affairs (Diyanet) and gives preferential status to Islam, particularly Sunni Islam.[10] Our empirical analysis indicates that the post-1923 absence of a state religion in Turkey—as we classify it—is a sharp outlier. Given Turkey's characteristics, the estimated probability of Turkey having a state religion in the long run turns out to be over 90 percent. This finding is consistent with the forces of Islamization that operate currently in Turkey under the

government of President Recep Tayyip Erdoğan. One clear indicator of the trend back toward an Islamic state religion is Turkey's recent elevation of the Directorate of Religious Affairs to the level of
a cabinet ministry. In fact, the annual budget of this office now
dwarfs that of education. Probably Turkey should already be classified as having a de facto Islamic state religion in 2018.

The results are different for the effects on state religion from the
presence of different types of Christians—for example, the large
numbers of Catholics and Protestants living in Germany. In this
case, a division among types of Christians makes it much less likely
that a state religion will prevail.

Why would a large share of Muslims in a country make a state
religion likely, even when these Muslims are of different types,
whereas representation by many different types of Christians has
the opposite effect? One point is that most Muslims agree that the
state bureaucracy is an extension of religious authority. In this
sense, the division between Sunni and Shia is secondary to the question of whether religious law and authority should govern society.
In contrast, with the creation of Protestantism with the Reformation of the 1500s, sharp religious and political competition between
Catholics and Protestants became central. These groups would never
agree on a Christian state religion that would somehow transcend
the differences between Catholics and Protestants.

We find in our research that the presence of state religion is not
much related to the level of economic development. Rich countries
—such as in Europe—and comparatively poor countries—such as in
Latin America or Africa—are similarly likely to have state religions.

Another finding is that, in the main range of country population
sizes (above around three million persons), the probability of state
religion diminishes as countries get larger. Our reasoning is that
large countries contain many people outside of the main religion
and therefore have large constituencies that counter the maintenance of a state-sponsored religious monopoly. India is a prominent
example here—the country is strongly majority Hindu but also features millions of Muslims and Christians and has no state religion.
Very small countries tend also not to have state religions, probably

because the cost of setting up a bureaucracy to maintain an official religion is not worth bearing. Thus, overall, there is an inverted-U relationship between the probability of state religion and the population of a country. Countries of intermediate size are the most likely to have a state religion.

We find that communist countries almost never had a state religion—when we do not view communism as its own religion. (The only exception was Somalia in the 1970s.) The key force here is the desire of communist leaders to prevent political competition from organized religion. One exception to the general pattern is that, although not constituting a state religion, the Catholic Church in Poland managed to sustain itself as an important counterforce against the communist government following World War II. As a general rule, the impact of past communism on the probability of having a state religion tends to diminish fairly quickly. Over the decade following the end of communist rule in the early 1990s, many countries—including Ukraine, Croatia, and several Central Asian republics—reinstated state religions.

Finally, we find that state religions have remarkable staying power over long periods. In countries that did not have a major regime change related to wars or communism or independence from a former colonial ruler, the probability of having a state religion in 2000 is highly correlated with whether a state religion existed in 1900. Thus, the long history reveals that state religions often last for hundreds of years. As mentioned before, in England, the current Anglican environment reflects King Henry VIII's ouster of the Catholic Church in 1534. Similarly, the long-lasting presence of the Lutheran state church in Sweden and the rest of Scandinavia stems from the ouster of the Catholic Church in Sweden by King Gustav Vasa in 1527.

In contrast, we have some evidence that not having a state religion is a less persistent condition than having one. We already noted that twelve countries that were forced to abandon state religion under communism—as parts of the Soviet Union or Yugoslavia— reinstated a state religion of various types soon after shedding the communist influence in the 1990s.

Who Is Right? Adam Smith versus David Hume on State Religion

As discussed in Chapter 2, state religion plays a central role in Adam Smith's (1791) vision of the religion market. According to Smith, the key aspect of an established religion, exemplified by the Anglican Church in England, is its promotion of the monopoly position of the favored religion. In many countries and time periods, this promotion occurs partly through limitations on entry by alternative religions and partly through subsidies of the favored religion.

Smith argued that a religion that relies upon the state, rather than its customers, tends to evolve in two ways. First, it tends to lose those aspects of religious devotion that are relevant to people practicing their faith and the authority of its doctrine. Second, it tends to become a religion for elites and, to the degree that the clergy itself becomes an elite group in society, of elites. Thus, instead of dedicating themselves to servicing the religious convictions of their congregants, the clergy tend to engage in secular activities such as politics, cultured activities such as the arts, and intellectual learning. Most importantly, having reached a position of state-ensured affluence, the clergy are not highly motivated to further the interests of their church members.

In contrast, Smith observed that alternative religions—in England called "upstarts"—depend on voluntary support from congregants. Therefore, these religions must continually address the religious needs of customers to stay in existence. As a consequence, the new religious movements, such as the Methodists and Quakers in England in the late 1700s, could successfully challenge the position of the Anglican Church by providing better and more tailored services. It was ingenious of Smith, who wrote the foundational book on the free market and the invisible hand (*The Wealth of Nations*), to apply his market model to religious goods and services as if they were analogous to brands of toothpaste.

Smith's argument helps us to understand the competition between Protestantism and Catholicism that arose with the Reformation in Europe in 1517. Robert Ekelund, Robert Hébert, and Robert

Tollison (2002; 2006, chaps. 5–7) observe that the Catholic Church was a monopolistic provider of services such as indulgences (forgiveness of temporal punishment for a sin) and simony (buying or selling of church offices). They argue that the Church had maintained high prices for its services by restricting entry, using methods such as excommunication and Inquisitions. The Church labeled competitors as "heretics" and dismissed magic and superstition—possibly rival supernatural forces—as invalid.

Ekelund, Hébert, and Tollison even contend that the Catholic Confessional was a mechanism for gaining information about individuals' willingness to pay for Church services, thereby allowing the Church to charge higher prices to persons who were more willing to pay. However, they also argue that the Church was so profitable that it attracted a lot of attempted entry despite the many roadblocks that the Church had erected. The Protestant Reformation that began in 1517 is a powerful case of successful entry. Notably, this new form of religion limited monopoly pricing by diminishing the intermediary role of Church professionals particularly when it came to indulgences, eliminating the Confessional, and emphasizing the potential for salvation through good works or predestination, rather than through services bought from the Church.

One argument from Smith, which forms the basis for the religion-market model that we discussed in Chapter 2, is that monopoly of religion tends to diminish religious participation and beliefs. Another point is that to counter the rise of competitor religions, the state religion tends to use coercion, repression, and even violence to maintain its favored status. This vision accords with the Catholic Church's responses to the rise of Protestantism after the Reformation of 1517. In its Counter-Reformation, originating from the Council of Trent of 1545 to 1563, the Catholic Church often relied on violence to counter the Protestant threat. It was not until the end of the Thirty Years' War with the Peace of Westphalia in 1648 that the long period of religious warfare in Europe came to an end. According to this peace agreement, the rulers of the German states were able to determine the religion of their lands among the options of Catholicism, Lutheranism, and Calvinism. Moreover, Christians living in principalities where their denomination was not the established religion were guaranteed the right to practice their own faith.

As with other sectors, Smith argued that the religion market is more vibrant where there is a disassociation between church and state. The absence of a monopoly state religion allowed for competition and, Smith believed, helped to create a society in which a great variety of religious faiths were able to flourish. Further, he thought that this pluralistic environment would feature rational discussion about religious beliefs and, thereby, create an atmosphere of "good temper and moderation." In contrast, with a state-sponsored monopoly of religion, Smith predicted that the attempted imposition of ideas on the public would lead to zealousness, violence, and little enthusiasm about religion.

Nineteenth-century Scottish philosopher David Hume's approach to church-state relations contrasts sharply with that of Adam Smith, although they were good friends. Hume (1998; 2006, pp. 75–80) argued that religion was simply superstition based on human fear of the unknown and anxiety over future uncertainties: "We hang in perpetual suspense between life and death, health and sickness, plenty and want; which are distributed amongst the human species by secret and unknown causes whose operation is oft unexpected and always unaccountable. These *unknown causes* then become the object of our hope and fear" (Hume 2006, p. 142). Thus, Hume's argument is that fear and anxiety motivate people to hold irrational beliefs in imaginary gods, rituals, charms, and relics. These irrational religious beliefs were viewed as psychological, brutish palliatives for what people cannot rationally explain: "You will scarcely be persuaded that they are other than sick men's dreams; or perhaps will regard them more as the playsome whimsies of monkeys in human shape than the serious, positive, dogmatical asseverations of a being who dignifies himself with the name of rational" (Hume 2006, p. 184). Hume did not distinguish a nonverifiable belief in an invisible god from superstitious beliefs, such as in the predictive power of horoscopes and fortune tellers, which can be readily verified as false.

The Humean view of religion as nonscientific, irrational, and motivated by fear and anxiety was also espoused much later by Sigmund Freud (1964a), the founder of psychoanalysis, who described belief in God as a collective neurosis: he called it "longing for a father." However, toward the end of his life, Freud (1964b) became more favorably disposed toward religion. He argued that because nonverifiable beliefs in concepts such as heaven and hell depended on a degree of imagination, it was plausible that more educated and scientific people would be more religious: "If people can worship what is not there, they can also reflect on what is not there, or on what is presented to them in symbolic and not immediate terms. So the mental labor of monotheism prepared the Jews ... to achieve distinction in law, in mathematics, in science and in literary art. It gave them an advantage in all activities that involved making an abstract model of experience." The older Freud called this internalizing process an "advance in intellectuality," and he credited it to religion.

For Hume, it was not a stretch to go from his vision of religion as irrational to the policy conclusion that the state ought to regulate the religion market to protect its citizens from being duped and preyed upon. Hume argued that religion leads to strife and violence and, therefore, that the state should regulate religion. According to Hume, "Those who undertake the most criminal and dangerous enterprises are commonly the most superstitious." And, for Hume, religion was not just harmless superstition. It was a source of conflict.

We can find examples of Hume's view in contemporary societies and events. In Sri Lanka, for example, Theravada Buddhism is the religion of the majority and is legally protected as well as promoted by the state. One of the state's constitutional obligations is to foster the Buddha *sasana*, or teaching of the Buddha. Since monks and their monastic communities are the teachers and perpetuators of Buddhism, they receive state subsidies.

While Buddhism is the preferred religion of the majority of Sri Lankans (around 70 percent), the country's constitution guarantees religious freedom. As a result, Christianity (in the forms of Catholicism, Anglicanism, and Mainline Protestantism), Hinduism, and Islam are legally recognized by the government. All other religious groups, such as evangelicals, pentecostals, and Assemblies of God, register as corporations. The result of this approach to religion has been to create a legally stratified religion market along with an informal, unregulated religion market.

Despite the apparent legal protections for minority religions, violent acts against evangelical, pentecostal, and Assemblies of God congregations have occurred frequently in Sri Lanka. In several cases, monks directed the violence against minority religionists. What is striking about these actions is that the majority of them are perpetrated by civil society, not the government. However, the national government has often failed to enforce the freedom of worship protected by the country's constitution, and religious strife has gone unchecked.

Hume would have pointed to Sri Lanka's religious conflict as evidence of his view that religion creates fanaticism and exclusivity, leading to disagreement and escalating into violence. One could reach the logical extension of Hume's argument that intolerance, left unregulated, is human nature.

There are other cases that support Hume's perspective on religion. With the fall of communism, religious missionary groups entered the five Central Asian countries of Kazakhstan, Kyrgyzstan, Uzbekistan, Turkmenistan, and Tajikistan. The governments sought to control the politicization of Islam, which is the dominant religion in these countries. At the same time, by focusing on Islam, they overlooked other religions that came in after the fall of communism. Initially, in the early 1990s, Turkmenistan and Uzbekistan were tolerant of evangelical and pentecostal groups on the grounds that religious tolerance was part of the "new republic." However, these countries moved later to regulate or even prohibit the rival religions.

By the mid-1990s, the new religious groups were not accepted by traditional religionists. There are several reasons for this behavior. First, the traditional religion, in this case Islam, saw the newcomers as taking away parishioners, along the lines of the religious competition that developed in Europe during the Reformation. Second, increasing strife occurred because of the crossing of ethnic and communal lines while engaging in proselytizing activities. Third, the new religious groups disregarded traditional customs and were viewed accordingly as disrespectful to one's ancestors.

The Central Asian countries, as well as Sri Lanka, are cases in which the government opted for increasingly restrictive legislation and administrative solutions to the civil tensions that religious pluralism introduced into society. Sri Lanka, like other countries, has considered banning types of proselytizing in order to restore social stability. The trend of reinforcing state control over religion through heavy regulation tends to be the result of religious leaders and politicians promoting a religious-nationalistic and, in some cases, ethnic agenda.

Hume contended that moral education would make religion unnecessary in that people would overcome their anxiety and fears through habit and moral ordering of their relations. He also argued that scientific discoveries and explanations of natural events would eliminate ignorance and hence the need for religion. However, this view conflicts with cross-country data, in that higher levels of education are not inversely correlated with indicators of religiosity (as we noted in Chapter 2).

We discussed in Chapter 2 how the existence of a state religion affects attendance at formal religious services and the intensity of various religious beliefs. In that analysis, we distinguished two aspects of state religion. One is the subsidy to the main religion; our expectation is that this element would lead to more participation at formal religious services. (When something is subsidized and its price falls, the quantity demanded tends to rise.) However, the effect on religious beliefs would be weak if the main religion provides poor and unconvincing services to its constituents.

The second consideration is regulation of the religion market, particularly the creation of legal impediments to the entry and growth of competitors to the principal religion. (In practice, we used a specific measure of regulation—whether government approval or direct governmental selection was required for the appointment of religious leaders.) Our expectation is that this force—sometimes but not always associated with state religion—would lead to less participation in formal religious services. Religious beliefs would tend also to fall if the presence of an array of competing religion providers were important in fostering beliefs.

The empirical findings discussed in Chapter 2 accord with these hypotheses. The existence of a state religion (for a given status of regulation of the religion market) tends to raise participation in formal religious services but lacks significant explanatory power for religious beliefs. In contrast, greater regulation of the religion market (for a given status of state religion) tends to depress religious participation and forms of religious beliefs.

What Do We Know about State Religion?

The theme of this chapter is the title of a 2005 article of ours, "Which Countries Have State Religions?" We care about the answer to this question particularly because, as shown in Chapter 2, state religion matters for religious participation (though not so much for religious beliefs). Moreover, we found in Chapter 3 that religious participation (and religious beliefs) matters for economic growth.

We classified most of the countries in the world on a de facto basis as to whether they had a state religion. In 2000, 75 out of 188 countries (40 percent) had a state religion, compared with 111 out of 188 (59 percent) in 1900. Thus, the overall trend in the propensity of countries to have a state religion was negative during the twentieth century. However, little change has occurred in this propensity since 1970, including from 2000 to today.

The strongest empirical pattern is that state religion is much more likely when the share of the adhering population belonging to the main religion is high. This pattern arises pretty much independently of which religion is the main one, although there is a small additional positive effect when the main religion is Islam. We find that a state religion is highly likely when most of the population is Muslim even when the population is fairly evenly split among types, such as between Shias and Sunnis in Iraq. On this point, in the next chapter we look at the historical distribution of Mahayana Buddhism in Tibet, beginning in the twelfth century. The initial pattern of multiple Buddhist schools evolved ultimately into a concentrated administration centered on the office of the Dalai Lama.

We found that Turkey's lack of a state religion (as has been true since the establishment of the Turkish Republic in 1923) is a strong outlier. We also found that for predominantly Christian countries that are fairly evenly split among types—Catholics, Protestants, and others—state religion is highly unlikely.

We find that higher economic development, gauged by real per capita GDP, has no explanatory power for the existence of a state religion. In contrast, a state religion is most probable for countries of intermediate population size. Countries with very high populations, such as India, tend not to have a state religion because of the countervailing pressure from the large number of minority religionists, such as Muslims and Christians in India. Small countries tend not to have a state religion because the limited scale does not warrant the administrative costs. Communist countries almost never have a state religion. However, once communism is given up, as for many countries at the start of the 1990s, there are many reinstatements of state religions. Thus, the impact of communism on the probability of state religion dissipates quickly over time.

State religions have remarkable duration. For example, it still matters today that state religions were established in England and Scandinavia during the Protestant Reformation that began in 1517. In fact, the split between the Christian and Orthodox churches in 1054 still influences today's patterns of state religion in some regions. And we saw, in Chapter 3, how the presence of a monopolistic religion in a geographic region, such as a Swiss canton, continues to influence people's attitudes toward work and leisure.

Although we discussed some effects from a country's having a state religion or regulating the religion market, it would be great if future research elaborated on these influences. As examples, we would like to know more about how state religion and religious regulation interact with religious freedom and with the maintenance more broadly of civil liberties and democratic governance.

6

Religious Clubs,
Terrorist Organizations,
and Tibetan Buddhism

What do religious cults such as the Unification Church, nicknamed the Moonies, the Islamic State of Iraq and Syria (ISIS), or the Dalai Lama's Geluk brand of Mahayana Buddhism have in common?[1] According to the economist Laurence Iannaccone's (1992) club model of religion, they are all forms of clubs that thrive by insisting on extreme behavior and sacrifice to promote homogeneity and commitment among members. The sacrifice and stigma screen out free riders and retain the enthusiastic participants who promote individual and group interests.

Some religions require costly practices. For example, adherents may have to dress in specified ways or be required to have facial hair or cover their heads. These behaviors are called stigmata because they signal to outsiders the allegiance to a group. Religions may also include sacrifices, such as prohibitions on eating specified foods, dedication of large amounts of time to religious practices, limitations on sexual and cohabitation practices (for example, celibacy for Catholic priests and Buddhist monks), as well as male and fe-male circumcision. One might have thought that these kinds of prac-tices would be eliminated by competition among religions. That is, in a modified version of Gresham's Law (normally applied to cheap money driving out good money), lax religions ought to force strict ones out of the market. This prediction is clearly wrong.

Religions with different degrees of strictness and costly rituals coexist in a competitive marketplace. But why is it that costly—and sometimes seemingly pointless—religious practices can have good survival characteristics? Iannaccone's (1992) club model explains this pattern by noting that stigma and self-sacrifice and engage-ment in unconventional behavior can make the group unappealing to less enthusiastic candidates and, thereby, eliminate free riders.[2] Iannaccone applied his framework to explain the existence of cults and sects that require extreme behavior by their members.[3] But the setting has much broader application.

Iannaccone's insight is that religious practice is a social (or club) experience, where people value associations with others who share their commitment and enthusiasm. In this setting, stigma and sac-rifice serve as signals of the extent of one's adherence to the sect. In practice, the costs of belonging can cover a wide range of actions: apparel and grooming, no jewelry (stigmas), as well as no elec-tronics, limiting educational attainment, and using only animals for agriculture and transportation (sacrifices). A key point is that the least committed members are the ones who react to the restrictions by defecting, thereby leaving behind the persons with the greatest enthusiasm and loyalty to the sect. Thus, although the costly prac-tices are, indeed, costly in themselves, they may be a price worth paying to ensure a more homogeneous, dedicated membership. Iannaccone's club model therefore provides a rational explanation for strict or extreme behavior that other academic fields such as psychology and anthropology tend to categorize as brainwashing or pathological behavior.

The description of a religious group as an enthusiastic social or-ganization also appears in the analysis of religion by the sociologist

Émile Durkheim ([1915] 2008). In Durkheim's setting, as in Iannaccone's, an individual's religious experience is more rewarding if a person is joined by others in the acts of praying, singing, taking part in processions and pilgrimages, and so on. Durkheim called these group activities "a state of effervescence," whereby the jointness of the participation meant "passions more active, sensations stronger" (p. 422). Communally performed rituals, rites, and ceremonies reaffirm a group's identity and strengthen emotional and psychological bonds.

Later in this chapter, we apply the club model of religious sects to the development of Tibetan Buddhism beginning in the twelfth century. The Geluk sect, of which the Dalai Lama is a member, rose to become the Tibetan state religion in 1642. This sect was one of the last to form in a crowded Buddhist religion market. Unlike the older sects, the Gelukpa introduced strictness by adhering to an orthodox version of Buddhism prescribed by the sect's theological canon. The sect required "sacrifice" in terms of individual morality (celibacy for monks, no alcohol) and religious practice (adhering to the 235 Vinaya precepts). The monks were required to reside in large monastic institutions, which excluded lay abbots, thereby minimizing involvement in secular politics.

The Gelukpa were more successful than other Mahayana Buddhist schools and sects in excluding the hereditary-succession practices for school leadership that underlay the usual clan politics. Instead, they created a corporate monastic system. With this organizational structure, the Geluk school was able to maintain institutional independence from kinship politics. Building on its institutional strengths and innovative theology, this school created a religious brand by differentiating itself from the existing forms. These advantages, when combined with the support of (foreign) Mongol patrons, allowed the Gelupka to establish Tibet's Buddhist state religion in the seventeenth century. Given the conventional view of Buddhism as highly peaceful, it is surprising that the process by which the Geluk sect became the Tibetan state religion featured monastic involvement by several sects in violence.[4]

The Club Model of Religion

Taking inspiration from the German theologian Ernst Troeltsch's analysis of sects and denominations, Iannaccone developed his club model of cost-induced commitment to organized religion.[5] He argued that people sometimes choose to undergo stigma and sacrifice that entails engaging in unconventional behavior with the purpose of eliminating free riders, thereby increasing the commitment of believers. Implicit in this structure is that people value contact with serious coreligionists. As an example, people like to sing in church along with others who sing enthusiastically rather than acting as free riders who sit on their hands. Thus, there is an incentive to screen out free riders, and strict practices—even if costly, per se— sometimes work effectively.

Radical religious sects are particularly efficient at attracting individuals who are willing to commit extreme acts in the name of religion because of the spiritual goods that only the group can provide and make available to members. Religion is a social phenomenon in that participating in activities such as the liturgy, singing, and praying together gives members satisfaction. Satisfaction is achieved through group participation, not individual consumption. The problem of free riding arises when individuals can benefit from a religion's public goods without having to contribute much themselves. One solution to this problem is to raise the requirements of belonging to the sect. This strictness then becomes a mechanism for ensuring cohesion of the group's members, thereby increasing homogeneity and levels of participation in collective activities. This mechanism works because the least enthusiastic participants are close to the margin of belonging to a religion and are, therefore, the most sensitive to the costs of strictness. In this case, imposing strictness induces nonserious people to depart, leaving behind a comparatively homogenous group of committed participants.

Strictness can take the form of sacrifices and prohibitions (stigmas). Examples include bans on leisure activities such as dances, movies, computer games, and gambling; prohibitions against alcohol,

tobacco, and caffeinated drinks; and specified diets and dress. Social stigmas make it costly (even impossible) to engage in activities
outside the group. Wearing distinct clothing, adopting unconventional hair styles (head and facial), and wearing head coverings stig-
matize a person and thereby reinforce her commitment to avoid
the outside world.

Stigma also takes the form of nonconformist religious practices. For example, the worship services of the early pentecostals in
the United States featured members making animal sounds such as
barking, howling, hooting like an owl, and chattering like a fright-
ened monkey. Pentecostal services were also characterized by laugh-
ing, moaning, speaking in gibberish (later identified as speaking in
tongues), shouting, screaming, and shrieking.[6] These enthusiastic
worship services drove the less committed away. Consequently, the
quantity and quality of within-group religious goods increased.

Jean-Paul Carvalho (2013) argues that veiling—meaning forms
of head covering and dress worn by Muslim women—may operate
differently from the distinctive clothing emphasized in usual club
models of religion. He notes a marked increase (the *new veiling
movement*) in the practice of veiling since the 1970s, particularly
among educated, middle-class Muslim women who live and work
in urban areas. He argues that this practice does not fit with Iannaccone's club model, in which distinctive dress would be a stigma that
signals to society a type of religious adherence. Rather, he argues
that the veil allows women from religious communities to participate effectively in irreligious environments, such as secular cities,
while simultaneously maintaining adherence to Islam. His argument
is that the veil is a commitment device that helps women avoid
temptation in irreligious settings and thereby allows them to maintain participation in and approval of their religious communities. In
his model, regulations on veiling—such as the French prohibition
on the wearing of head scarves in public schools and more compre-
hensive bans on full-face veils in several European countries—can
have perverse effects on the life choices of Muslim women. Notably,
these bans may increase religiosity and inhibit social integration.

An example of this mechanism is the May 2018 Dutch ban on the wearing of burqa and niqab, which followed the bans in France (2004, 2010, 2012) and Austria (2017). The Dutch ban does not include the hijab (which only covers the hair). These bans remove the stigma (burqa, niqab, hijab) from the public sphere. However, the bans also eliminate the corresponding benefit—providing a mechanism for Muslim women to engage with the majority host culture and its values. Consequently, the bans end up restricting the access of Muslim women to public goods, including secular education and employment, and setting them up for marriage at an early age. Although more research needs to be conducted on the effects of these bans on the lives of Muslim girls and women, a senator of the Green Party in the Netherlands observed that the ban has the effect of forcing many Muslim women to remain at home (Raf Casert and Aleksandar Furtula 2018).

Another consequence of these bans is that the stigma becomes a political symbol. Muslim women have come to interpret wearing the headscarf as an intentional ethno-religious identity choice and as a form of protest (Francoise Gaspard and Farhad Khosrokhavar 1995; Christine Delphy 2015). One study found far-reaching consequences of a ban. Alexandra Kassir and Jeffrey G. Reitz (2016) studied the effects of the French Ministry of Education's enactment in 2012 of the *Chatel circular*, which bans mothers from wearing head scarves during parental participation in school field trips. The mothers formed four separate activist groups to counter the ban. Based on interviews with these Muslim women, Kassir and Reitz found that they identified as French citizens, even though some had immigrated to France. The mothers interpreted their activism as asserting their political rights as French citizens. The ban created a dichotomy between their religious beliefs and community and their French identity. The mothers distanced themselves from the imams as well as Muslim organizations, contending that wearing a headscarf was a personal choice, not a religious or patriarchal one. The government ban on wearing of headscarves had an effect opposite to that of stigma in the standard club model. Rather than reinforcing

Muslim group exclusivity, the ban brought into sharp relief the mothers' political identify as French citizens, thereby turning a religious stigma into a political symbol of integration into French society.

The core business of a religious club rests on its capacity to maintain credibility and minimize free riding. These attributes facilitate mutual insurance, philanthropy, and community action. Credibility is critical in business dealings, trading networks, and social-service provision. Thus, we should not be surprised to see religious clubs successfully engaged in these activities, especially where weak government or civil disorder undermines the secular provision of schooling, health care, antipoverty programs, rule of law and property rights, physical security in the form of police protection, and so forth. In the French case, the credibility of the Muslim community, particularly the authority of the imams to defend a mother's right to wear a headscarf on field trips, was weak vis-à-vis the state.

In addition to spiritual goods, a religious club supplies material goods that can be received only by joining and belonging to the group. Moreover, these clubs provide mutual aid, which we discuss in more depth in the next section on violent religious groups. This feature distinguishes religious clubs from for-profit organizations, such as firms and drug cartels. The religious club also differs from nonprofit organizations that seek outside donations and assist strangers. Members sustain the religious club through labor, tithing, subsidies, and forms of taxation. These clubs flourish because they provide their members with material and spiritual benefits for the present, extreme beliefs about the future, and insurance against misfortune.

By now, the club model has been used in many contexts, going beyond religious groups. For a survey of these applications, see Jason Aimone et al. (2013). They note that the sacrifice/stigma mechanism works particularly well when standard methods of group selection— such as membership fees, usage tolls, and selective expulsion—are costly or illegal. They also study how the posited sacrifice mechanism operates in lab experiments that allow participants to choose their levels of contributions to a club.

Violent Religious Groups

The club model was extended by the economist Eli Berman to explain why people join violent religious sects and terrorist groups.[7] In this model, violent religious groups can be effective because they are motivated by an uncompromising faith that justifies horrendous acts against opponents and rationalizes extreme self-sacrifice, including suicide attacks. Surprisingly, however, the research on violent religious groups by Eli Berman (2009) and Vera Mironova (2017) found that a theological explanation is inconsistent with the evidence. For example, failed suicide attackers, when interviewed, seldom cite religion as their primary motivation. Moreover, the Palestinian Islamic jihad and Hamas share almost identical theologies, yet the latter is much deadlier than the former when judged by the number of fatalities per attack.

If religious beliefs and doctrine are not the answer, why are religious radicals so effective at violence? Berman (2009) contends that the explanation lies in the internal economies of the organizations these militants and terrorists grew out of. What the most successful radical Islamic militant and terrorist organizations have in common is a strong faith-based infrastructure of social-service provision through mutual aid. Though the connection between mutual aid and violence seems surprising on an ethical level, from an organizational perspective it makes perfect sense. Berman's application of the club model to violent groups became known as the Hamas model. The distribution of goods and services by this radical, religious, and violent group is done in exchange for allegiance to the group (Berman 2009, p. 132).

Berman found that the mutual aid model is most effective in countries or regions with inefficient if not failed economies. Radical religious groups that engage in violence, such as Hamas, the Taliban, Hezbollah, and al-Sadr's militia, thrive in inefficient economies as they rely on members who have poor outside alternatives to joining the group. Should outside options exist, these groups ensure that they destroy them. That is why many of these groups have a scorched earth approach to warfare.

Mironova (2017) conducted field research on Islamic rebel groups in Syria and found that the country's failing economy during the civil war meant that rebel groups assumed an array of responsibilities for fighters and their families. The Syrian war was fought by numerous rebel groups sharing the same goal: the overthrow of President Bashar al-Assad's regime. There were numerous violent Islamic groups on the other side fighting for the al-Assad regime. As a result, fighters could choose not only which side to fight on but which rebel group to join.

Among the numerous Islamic rebel groups in the Syrian civil war, Jabhat al-Nusra and Ahrar al-Sham appear to be the most successful. ISIS, consisting mostly of foreign fighters, entered the civil war later with the goal of establishing the Islamic State, a regional caliphate. Jabhat al-Nusra and Ahrar al-Sham, composed of Syrian rebel groups, shared the goal of overthrowing al-Assad. Al-Nusra and al-Sham increased their share of power within the rebel opposition bloc relative to the other groups through their mutual aid programs. Benefits included food, housing, clothing, health care, a regular stipend (sometimes paid in cash or valued goods such as meat and vegetables), military training, weapons and ammunition, and support staff to repair weapons and vehicles. The long-term support relied on by fighters included medical care for the wounded, postmortem arrangements for deceased fighters, and financial support for families (widows and children). Strong mutual aid programs ensured the loyalty and commitment of fighters. Fighters were able to focus on their goal (succeeding on the battlefield) without being preoccupied with how to provide for themselves and their families. Mironova, like Berman, found that reliable mutual aid programs provided by rebel groups freed fighters to take more risks in combat and, as a result, become a deadlier fighting group.

Protestant Christian radical sects, such as the Amish, Mennonites, Hutterites, and Shakers, as well as the Quakers and Methodists during the Industrial Revolution in England, did not use violence to express their grievances. If we conceptualize Protestant nonviolent sects at one end and violent Islamic sects at the other end of a continuum, then we can argue that both extremes rely on the club model of mutual aid and provision of public goods. Why don't some of these radical sects engage in violence? To consider this question, we introduce two additional aspects of religious sects: (1) theology/doctrine/moral beliefs and (2) external threats real or perceived by the sect to its survival or worldview.

In terms of theology, beliefs professed by members of a religious sect are themselves acts of cohesion. These shared beliefs signal to outsiders the commitment of members to the group. The societal rejection of the group's extremist beliefs makes the group all the more attractive to members. "The fact that belief is extreme and difficult to rationalize on ordinary criteria is part of its attraction" (Ronald Wintrobe 2006, p. 151). This statement is true as much for pacifist groups as for violent ones.

On the issue of external real or perceived threats, pacifist radical religious sects for the most part are embedded in functioning market economies, whereas violent sects are embedded in inefficient if not failed economies. For the Protestant sects we mentioned earlier, the national market works for them. They benefit from a functioning economy, and these religious groups emphasize the positive aspects of belonging: trust, lower divorce rates (marital stability), education for their children (even if it is sectarian and homeschooled), improved physical and mental health, and higher levels of happiness and fulfillment.

Ran Abramitzky (2008, 2018) applied Iannaccone's insights and Berman's Hamas model to Israel's kibbutzim. Like Berman, Abramitzky interprets ideology as an instrumental characteristic of a group, in other words, as a means to an end and not the end itself. As the socialist egalitarian ideology on which Israeli kibbutzim were originally founded lost relevance in an increasingly prosperous Israel, those with better outside prospects for employment left, creating a brain drain. The higher educated and skilled members exited, leaving the kibbutzim with less productive members, thereby lowering the standard of living.

Some radical religious sects might become violent *primarily because of their fragility* due to difficult economic and social conditions or due to persecution. This causation is inherent in the commonly held view that religious violence occurs because of poverty and high-income inequality. However, Alan Krueger and Jitka Maleckova (2003) challenge this view. They find that suicide bombers tend to be relatively well educated and do not come from the poorer segments of society. Islamic terrorists, such as those affiliated with Hamas and Hezbollah, are most likely to be middle class, with relatively high levels of educational attainment. Krueger and Maleckova speculate that high educational attainment may "signal one's commitment to a cause and determination, as well as one's ability to prepare for an assignment and carry it off.... We suspect their primary motivation results from their *passionate support* for their movement" (2003, p. 123, emphasis added). They also cite other studies with similar conclusions and contend that violent religious groups may prefer educated, middle- or upper-class individuals because as terrorists they are capable of carrying out a calculated plan while holding an extreme club-shared belief.

According to Hussein Mussawi, a founding member of Hezbollah, a Shia Islamist militant group and political party based in Lebanon, expressed it, "We are not fighting so that the enemy recognizes us and offers us something. We are fighting to wipe out the enemy." Hence, the constituency is not only self-referring (oneself and one's community of believers) but the position is absolutist. Religious terrorists tend to view violence as an end, not a means to political or economic ends. The secular terrorist views violence as a way to attain stated objectives, such as the overthrow of the government. For the religious terrorist, the situation calls for no compromise—"Our attitude is dictated by our religious beliefs"—whereas the secular terrorist is utilitarian (costly violence as a means to an end).

The religious terrorist perceives himself or herself as engaging in the destruction of a system with which he or she does not identify. The problem lies with the enemy, not with the sect. Krueger (2007) defines this alienation not in religious terms but in political and economic ones. In his research, he found that deterioration in economic conditions over time is associated with the likelihood of educated men becoming terrorist attackers. For example, during the 1980s, unemployment rose dramatically in the West Bank and

Gaza Strip for college graduates, relative to high school graduates. Therefore, the increase in educational attainment in the 1980s coincided with a marked deterioration in the economic opportunities for educated Palestinians, particularly males. Moreover, the loss in employment was attributed by Palestinians to the Israelis and the political situation.

In assessing the connection between human capital and the propensity to become a terrorist, we should keep in mind that this capital is useful in the ordinary economy and also in the terrorist environment. Thus, when employment opportunities worsen in the regular economy, the balance in the usefulness of human capital shifts toward terrorism. In other words, the person most likely to become a terrorist is not the one with the least human capital. Rather, it is the one with the most underutilized human capital. High education and lack of "legitimate" employment opportunities are a toxic mixture with respect to facilitating terrorism.

This argument is analogous to the one discussed in Chapter 2, where Binzel and Carvalho (2017) found that the Islamic revival in Egypt starting in the early 1980s was driven by educated youth. As in Krueger (2007), the key matter is that the expanded education was not matched by job opportunities that utilized the greater human capital.

Of course, economic calculations are not the only element in a person's willingness to become a terrorist. Krueger (2007) observes that terrorist activity on the part of educated males is a response to political conditions and long-standing feelings of indignation and frustration that become fueled by religious beliefs that legitimate and justify violence. Individuals join radical religious groups seeking to maintain a sense of self-respect, to have group support, and to gain a sense of belonging (identity). Krueger's research shows that prior to joining a radical religious sect, individuals had established political identities and were active members of society. Their commitment to a radical religious sect and the performance of violent acts of terrorism was typically a gradual process.

Mironova (2017) found that, as the Syrian civil war continued, Islamic ideologies changed with succeeding generations of fighters. When new fighters joined a rebel group, they brought along knowledge about the ongoing civil war and the various rebel groups involved in the fighting. Some fighters became religiously radicalized, interpreting the goal of the group to be religious (ideological) rather than overthrowing al-Assad. These radicalized fighters challenged the internal dynamics of the rebel group, some going so far as to challenge the religiosity of the leadership, calling them *kafirs* (infidels). Mironova's research shows that as an armed conflict drags on for years, religion can play a radicalizing role, permeating the language, thinking, activities, and goals of a group.

How does an Islamic rebel group ensure that ideology does not become radicalized to the point that it causes the destruction of the group? Vera Mironova, Ekaterina Sergatskova, and Karam Alhamad (2017) found that ISIS persecuted and killed radicalized fighters within its ranks. That policy was costly because ISIS was eliminating valuable fighters that the group had trained. Al-Nusra took a more moderate approach by establishing homogeneous groups, so that radicalized agents continued to fight but did not interact regularly with other fighters. As a rebel group, al-Nusra was clear in communicating the goal as the overthrow of al-Assad. The group's leadership encouraged fighters to educate themselves about Islam and one's faith, thereby promoting an open discussion as well as a positive view of Islam. Finally, as mentioned earlier, radicalized religious commitment became harder to maintain when material goods provided by a rebel group's mutual aid programs were scarce. As a civil war continues on for years, destroying a society to the point of being a failed state makes it easier for religion to become radicalized.

The Rise of the Geluk School Theocracy in Tibet

When we visited Tibet in 2005, we were struck by the vibrancy of the principal indigenous religion, Mahayana Buddhism. This enthusiasm persisted despite the Dalai Lama's exile status in Dharamsala, India, since 1959 and many decades of attempted suppression of Tibetan Buddhism by the Chinese government. Although Tibet has been described as the Tibet Autonomous Region since 1965, China has, in fact, sought to integrate Tibet into China through administration directed from Beijing, in-migration of many Han Chinese, and the completion of numerous economic development projects. These projects are a mixed blessing, on the one hand enhancing Tibetans' economic status, and on the other hand contributing to the decline of their traditional culture.

During our trip in 2005, we noticed that Tibetan religious expression in Lhasa included the daily practice of the *kora*, whereby pilgrims circumambulate up to 108 times inside the holy site of the Jokhang Temple and the outside perimeter of the Potala Palace. The kora pilgrims eagerly turn prayer wheels, count rosary beads, chant mantra, and continually prostrate themselves. And despite their typically low incomes, Tibetans frequently donated money at holy sites, for example, by sticking bills into metal fences that protected religious objects. It was clear that Buddhism was alive and well in Tibet.

We wondered how the supreme position of Tibetan Buddhism headed up by the Dalai Lama had come to be. To learn about this history, Rachel carried out research with her colleague, Leonard van der Kuijp (2010). It turned out that the elevation of the Dalai Lama's Geluk school of Tibetan Buddhism to become the state religion had origins going back to the fifteenth century. Surprisingly, given the usual view of Tibetan Buddhism as peaceful, the formation of this state religion involved a good deal of violence. We can use the club model to understand this process, particularly how a religious monopoly can be created and enforced through the willingness and ability of a successful competitor to engage in violence.

The Geluk school, of which the current (Fourteenth) Dalai Lama, Tenzin Gyatso, is an incarnate hierarch, competed in the fifteenth and sixteenth centuries with other Mahayana Buddhist schools. McCleary and van der Kuijp (2010) used the club model to argue that the club-like nature of religious groups explains why some Buddhist schools in Tibet were able to generate the extreme violence that led to the Gelukpa state religion in 1642.[8]

Over the eleventh and twelfth centuries, the ready availability of Indian ideas encouraged the formation of a diversity of Buddhist schools in Tibet (see Table 6.1). By the end of the twelfth century, Mahayana Buddhism constituted a relatively homogeneous religion market in Tibet. Within that market, four Buddhist schools and quasi-independent splinter sects developed with little differentiation in religious products. The schools and sects competed for patrons and novices. Each school tried to price its products above average costs to make a profit. In this market, a religious hierarch commanded a higher price than a less experienced monk for merit-making activities. The high prices encouraged young men to enter schools so as to be able eventually to garner wealthy patrons and adherents.

In the fourteenth century, the newly installed Ming dynasty (1368–1424) shifted China's foreign policy toward Tibet to one of nonintervention. This policy was a combination of concentrating resources on military campaigns in Southeast Asia and overseeing the extensive fourteen-year reconstruction of the capital of Beijing (Edward Dreyer 1982, pp. 173–220; Edward Farmer 1976, pp. 98–133). The consequence of China's reduced influence was a liberalization of local Tibetan politics with one major pattern emerging: a shift from secular politics and clan wealth to ecclesiastical monastic institutions.

The Geluk school was established in central Tibet during the Ming dynasty. The first Geluk monasteries—Ganden (1409), Drepung (1415), Dpal 'khor chos sde (1418), and Sera (1419)—were near the administrative centers of their patrons. What is significant about this pattern is that the other religious schools and sects were well established by the time the Geluk school began to form. Competition for resources in terms of patrons, land, and adherents was intense. By locating monasteries in geographic proximity to their patrons, the Geluk monasteries were assured of military protection and resources.

The Geluk school introduced innovative club features. Whereas other schools and sects allowed lay family members to become abbots of their monasteries, the Gelukpa were more successful in excluding the hereditary-succession practices for school leadership that underlay the usual clan politics. By permitting only ordained

TABLE 6.1. Lineages, Schools, and Sects in Tibetan Buddhism

Sakyapa School
Naropa (?–1040)
Drogmi Shakya Yeshe (ca. 993–1077)
Kon Kochog Gyelpo (1034–1102). Builds Sakya monastery in 1073
Zhalupa Sect
Jonangpa Sect
Ngorpa Sect
Dzongpa Sect
Tsharpa Sect
Kadampa School
Naropa
Atisha (ca. 982–1054) arrives in Tibet in 1042
Dromston Gyelway jungne (1004/1005–63/64). Builds Radreng monastery in 1056/1057
Kagyü School
Naropa and his disciple Maitripa
Marpa Lotsawa (1012?–1097?)
Milarepa (1038–1123)
Gampopa (1079–1153)
Tshal pa Sect
Karma Sect
Zhanag incarnation series
Zhamar incarnation series
Barom Sect
Phagmodru Sect
    a. Drigung Sect
    b. Staglung Sect
    c. Trophu Sect
    d. Drugpa Sect
    e. Marpa Sect
    f. Yelpa Sect
    g. Yabsang Sect
    h. Shugseb Sect
Gelukpa School
Tsongkapa (1357–1419). Builds Ganden Monastery in 1409
Dalai Lama incarnation series

From a longer version of a chart in Rachel M. McCleary and Leonard van der Kuijp, "The Market Approach to the Rise of the Geluk School, 1419–1642," *Journal of Asian Studies* (2010) 69, no. 1 (February), 149–180.

monks, the Gelukpa created a corporate monastic system. With this system, the Geluks reinforced an institutional focus on monastic religious activities and the collective monastic community.

The Geluk school required all monks, including the Dalai Lama, to belong to a monastery and to participate in communal activities.

Sacrifice of time was involved in participating in collective religious activities performed in the great hall at least once a day and twice during religious festivals. Geluk monasteries also required adherence to monastic discipline and morality including celibacy (the worst offenses were homicide, larceny, and heterosexual sex).

The principal structural features of the Geluk school were (1) monk abbots, never lay abbots; (2) an emphasis on monastic discipline (celibacy), moral (*vinaya*) adherence, and scholastic training; (3) doctrinal orthodoxy contained in the canon; and (4) mass monasticism, which created a competitive advantage in an already crowded and competitive religious market. The primary advantage of these club features was the emphasis on religious goods and minimization of the Geluk school's involvement in secular activities and clan politics, particularly conflicts over hereditary leadership.

The relationship between a wealthy politically connected patron and the Gelukpa was important given that the school did not permit lay family members to become abbots or assume administrative responsibility over its monasteries. In 1493, with the loss of its major Tibetan patron, the Gelukpa were confronted with serious competition from the Karmapa sect, patronized by the Rinpung, a relatively new aristocratic family vying for political control over central Tibet, the geographic region where the Gelukpa monasteries were concentrated.

At this critical period of its survival, the Geluk school introduced the incarnate position of the Dalai Lama and his *labrang* (financial estate). The introduction of the incarnate Dalai Lama facilitated the Gelukpa's competition for wealthy patrons, a much-needed source of spiritual authority and revenue. Incarnate lamas had already been a feature of the Karmapa sect. David Carrasco (1959, pp. 23–24) hypothesizes that the Gelukpa adopted this practice in order to solidify the school's independence from a single clan, thereby avoiding involvement in secular family politics. Melvyn Goldstein (1973, pp. 445–455) points out that the birth of an incarnate outside of the aristocracy triggered the circulation of land and tenant households from the aristocracy into religious institutions. Incarnates had their own personal labrangs in the form of land and goods, and these accumulated from one reincarnation to the next. Labrangs were corporate entities that, upon the death of a hierarch, were managed by designated stewards until the reincarnation was identified.

After the death of their major patron in 1493 and with no prospects of an aristocratic family to support them within central Tibet, the Geluk monasteries were under siege from the politically ambitious Karmapa sect supported by the Rinpung family. This conflict escalated with Lhasa overrun in 1498 by the Rinpung.

The Third Dalai Lama (1543–1588), lacking the means to rout the Karmapa from central Tibet, finally accepted an invitation from Altan Khan, chief of the Tümed Mongols. The visit to Mongolia in 1578 was primarily a strategic political move under the guise of religious proselytizing.[9] According to Zahiruddin Ahmad (1970, pp. 89–92), the Mongol chief converted to Geluk Buddhism and conferred upon the Third Dalai Lama the title of "Dalai." In exchange, the Third Dalai Lama conferred upon the Mongol Khan the title "the King according to the Faith, the Divine Mahā-Brahman."[10] The ancient pattern of patron-lama relationship was thereby reestablished, ensuring the expansion of Mongolian influence into Tibet and the spread of Geluk Buddhism into Mongolia and eastern Tibet, traditional Karmapa territory.

The religious following of the Geluk sect among the various Mongol chiefs and their tribes was critical to building the political base essential to the survival of the Geluk sect (Richardson 1962, p. 41). The Third Dalai Lama spent ten years in Inner Mongolia proselytizing among the various tribes (Hanzhang Ya [1991, p. 26]; Tsepon Shakabpa [1967, pp. 94–95]). The "proselytizing energy" of the Third Dalai Lama allowed him to garner in a short span of time the devotion of most of the Tumed, Chahar, and Khalkha Mongol tribes (Richardson 1958, p. 15; 1962, p. 41; Rolf Stein 1983). These Gelukpa contacts with Mongols would eventually increase tensions with the Karmapa sects.

The rebirth of the Third Dalai Lama in a grandson of Altan Khan raised the political-religious stakes for the Karmapa sects, which also claimed the Fourth Dalai Lama as one of their reincarnate lamas. In 1602, a large Mongolian escort brought the Fourth Dalai

Lama, then fifteen, from Inner Mongolia to Drepung Monastery near Lhasa. It appears that the Mongols were reluctant to have the Dalai Lama live in Tibet, but the abbots of the Geluk monasteries were concerned over the Lama's education and his potential deviation from monastic celibacy. Furthermore, we can speculate that, without the Dalai Lama in Tibet, the religious institutions of the Geluk school would be perceived as weak and vulnerable to outside attacks.

The Karmapa took steps to consolidate its authority over Tibet. From 1603 to 1621, Tibetan politics deteriorated into civil war. Taking advantage of the death of the Fourth Dalai Lama in 1615, the Tsang aristocratic family invaded Lhasa, and this time they were successful, killing several thousand monks at Sera and Drepung monasteries.[11]

In 1622, the Fifth Dalai Lama (1617–1682), the son of a Tibetan aristocratic family, was identified and brought as a young boy to a Geluk monastery in Lhasa. The Karmapa allied themselves with the Khalkha Mongols, who had conquered northeastern Tibet (Amdo region). The Khalkha Mongols prepared to send ten thousand troops to central Tibet to annihilate the Gelukpas once and for all. However, the Olot Mongols, accompanied by Geluk monks who had temporarily given up their vows to become fighters, defeated the Karmapa. Thus, in 1642, the Fifth Dalai Lama, with the military backing of Mongol tribes, claimed his secular and sacred authority over central Tibet.

The Geluk school, as the monopoly religion, made the state the legitimate interpreter of the Buddhist religion. To buttress its theocratic rule, only the Gelukpa were permitted to have monasteries in and around Lhasa (Graham Sandberg 1906, p. 106). The consequence of this arrangement between political authority and religion was the imposition of the Geluk school over the other Buddhist schools and sects. The Geluk state secured its hold on the religion market through government subsidies and special privileges to its own monasteries, such as the Dalai Lama permitting monasteries to conscript children of hereditary households, especially when the monastery needed novices. For smaller monasteries with few

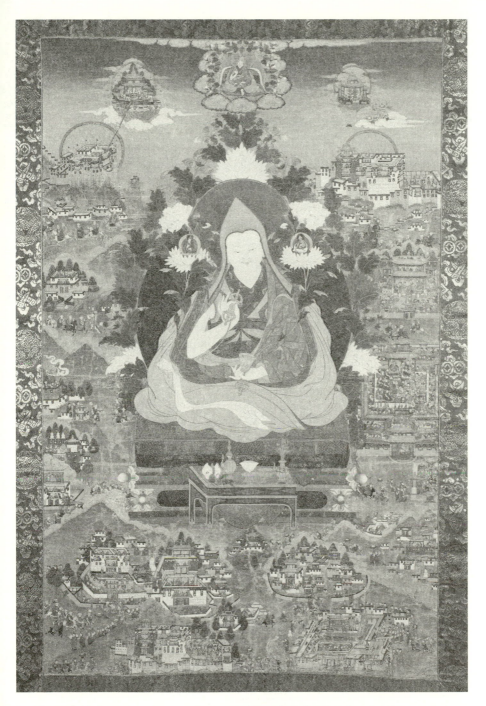

FIGURE 6.1. Fifth Dalai Lama. Scenes from *The Life of the Fifth Dalai Lama (1617–1682) Tibet 18th Century*. Pigments on cloth. Rubin Museum of Art C2003.9.2 (HAR 65275).

agricultural resources, the Dalai Lama instituted state subsidies in barley, butter, and tea. Eventually, the monasteries of the other schools and sects assumed institutional features of the Geluk monastic system, so much so that today it is difficult to discern how the other schools and sects might have functioned independently prior to the ascendancy of the Geluk as the state religion.

The rise of the Geluk school explains how, in the absence of a central political authority, religious groups with similar underlying theology—in this case, Mahayana Buddhism—will compete until one becomes dominant. Thus, the history of the rise of the Geluk school demonstrates that religious pluralism in the form of competing groups can be superseded by a monopoly religion.

As further testament to the monopolistic position that the Geluk school held over Tibetan Buddhism, by the late seventeenth century the religious-political history of Mongolian Buddhism was revised to be a Gelupka history. All other schools of Buddhism were considered advocating "wrong views" and were uniformly categorized as Karmapa (Karenina Kollmar-Paulenz 2018, p. 147).

Insights from the Club Model

Laurence Iannaccone's club model explains how religious groups can use costly admission requirements to form a dedicated membership. These requirements include stigma and self-sacrifice that are bearable only for committed adherents and, thereby, serve to screen out free riders. The homogeneous and serious adherents who remain enhance the social experience of members and make the club efficient at carrying out mutual aid. In the context of violent organizations, "clubs" can be effective at terrorism.

In analyzing the rise of the Geluk school as the Buddhist state religion in Tibet in the 1600s, we combined our research on state religion with the club model. A religion monopoly tends to arise naturally when there exists a strong concentration of adherents in a particular religion (Barro and McCleary 2005). As larger numbers of people adhere to one religion, more people are disposed toward that religion. People not only want to belong and have a shared liturgical experience but also want to share similar beliefs, doctrines, and worldviews. With many people adhering to a single faith, there is a tendency to form a religion monopoly. In particular, such concentration economizes on the fixed costs of maintaining a large variety of religion types. The Gelukpa religious monopoly is an example of this. The Geluk school arose from a pluralistic market with a uniformity of religious teachings based on Mahayana Buddhism with distinct emphases. Given the usual view of Buddhism as peaceful, the reality of intense and violent conflict up to the success of the Gelupka in a military climax in 1642 is surprising.

Although the club model is useful for many applications, we should note that it has limitations for an analysis of religion and economy. The model is fundamentally a theory of social organization, not an analysis of religion per se. Uniform religious beliefs may help to sustain an organization and may be central to the inclusion or exclusion of members. But the framework would apply equally well to other forms of ideology and club-like activities. In the model, religion is not special because of its reliance on nonverifiable supernatural beliefs or its focus on salvation, damnation, or forms of spiritual transmigration and miraculous abilities. In this context, we should recall our empirical findings from Chapter 3, whereby—in tune with Max Weber's ([1904–1905] 1930) vision of the Protestant ethic—religious beliefs, gauged relative to participation in formal services, was the main religion-based force that enhanced economic growth. The club model explains more about participation than about beliefs and, therefore, does not tell us much about Weber and the Protestant ethic.

7

When Saints Come Marching In

Some years ago, we were touring Antigua, the capital of Guatemala until 1776. We visited the San Francisco Church, where the remains of Hermano Pedro, Guatemala's only Roman Catholic saint, are located.[1] Hundreds of people waited a long time to see Pedro's tomb. Once there, people often approached the stately wood and iron casket on their knees, then prayed, placed flowers, and tied wax effigies of body parts for which they were seeking a miracle cure onto the metal grill encircling the tomb. Before leaving, the supplicants knocked on Hermano Pedro's tomb to ensure that he had heard their prayers.

Hermano Pedro was born in 1626 and later left his native Canary Islands to avoid an arranged marriage. He made his way to Guatemala, where he became a Franciscan, abiding by a threefold rule of simplicity, chastity, and obedience. Hermano Pedro chose to work among the ill, lame, prisoners, and orphans. In Antigua, he established a hospital and founded a new order, the Order of Bethlehemite Brothers, dedicated to providing health care for the indigent. In 1980, Pope John Paul II beatified Hermano Pedro and named him a saint in 2002. (As we discuss later, beatification is the first stage for becoming a saint, and canonization is the second stage.)

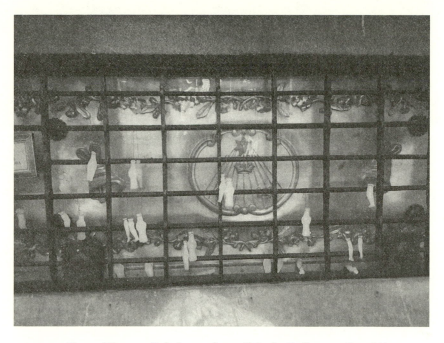

FIGURE 7.1. Photo of Hermano Pedro's mausoleum. Alejandro Farfán, www.Guate360.com.

In a country dominated by the growth of evangelical and pentecostal denominations and neo-pentecostal megachurches, the level of activity at the Catholic San Francisco Church surrounding Saint Hermano Pedro was an anomaly. In 1964, the last year the Guatemalan national census reported religious affiliation, 8.2 percent of Guatemalans were Protestant, with the majority adhering to evangelical and pentecostal faiths. In 2001, an estimated 30 percent of Guatemalans were Protestant; in 2007, their share was 36 percent; currently, it is around 40 percent.

Since the early twentieth century, the growth of *evangélicos*, as Protestants are referred to in Latin America, has been dramatic. In 1900, they comprised 2.6 percent of the Latin American population; they reached 17 percent by 2010 and 19 percent in 2014 (Pew Research Center 2014, p. 26). The growth of Protestantism in Latin America is in large part due to conversion from Catholicism. Proselytizing efforts by evangelicals and pentecostals are successful as they offer a personal approach to faith. The challenge for the current

Pope Francis I, himself a Latin American, is to stem the attrition from Catholicism by making the Church attractive to younger people who are primarily the ones switching to Protestantism. One way of making Catholicism more appealing is through the naming of saints.

We wondered whether the Catholic Church was using this strategy in Latin America but also promoting sainthood in other parts of the world to reinvigorate Catholic adherence. We decided to find out by pursuing a research project on the choices of saints going back to the sixteenth century. Our analysis explores whether the Church has found a way to compete effectively against the growing competition from Protestant evangelicals, especially in Latin America. We found evidence for this competitive response through increased saint making, and we were able to put numbers on how important it has become.

The Catholic Church's Competitive Response to Protestantism

After centuries of Italian popes, from 1523 to 1978, the Catholic Church's College of Cardinals elected three consecutive non-Italians. The appointments of John Paul II from Poland (in office 1978–2005), Benedict XVI from Germany (2005–2013), and Francis I from Argentina (2013–) reflect the Church's increasingly global orientation.

Pope John Paul II, the first non-Italian Pope since Hadrian VI (1522–1523), beatified a remarkable 319 individuals as confessors (the category of ordinary saints, which excludes martyrs). This number beatified by John Paul II exceeded the combined total of 259 from all of his thirty-six predecessor popes back to 1590. Popes Benedict XVI and Francis I through 2017 continued the rapid pace of beatification—with 92 and 46, respectively. When expressed per year in office, John Paul II's beatification rate was 12.0 per year, Benedict XVI's was 11.7, and Francis I's (through 2017) was 9.6. These numbers sharply exceeded the average of 0.5 per year that applied to the thirty-six popes from 1590 to 1978.

The shift to internationalize the Catholic Church shows up in the composition of beatifieds. The traditional pattern for centuries focused on persons from Italy and the rest of Western Europe. At least by the early 1900s, a geographic broadening of beatification began to encompass Eastern Europe, Latin America, North America, Asia, and Africa. We attribute these changes to religious competition with Protestants in what historically were Catholic countries.

In terms of numbers and based on a person's residence at death, Italy accounted for 56 percent of new blessed persons (beatifieds) from 1590 to 1899, compared to 42 percent from 1900 to 2012. The percentage for other Western Europe stayed fixed at 33 percent, but other regions went up. Latin America went from 6 to 8 percent, Eastern Europe from 4 to 7 percent, North America from 0 to 5 percent, Asia from 1 to 4 percent, and Africa from 0 to 2 percent. This geographical spread means that many countries received their first saint only recently. Aside from Guatemala, countries with first-time saints in the 2000s include Mexico, Brazil, Sudan, Ukraine, Ireland, Malta, India, Australia, and Belarus.

The spread of newly named blessed persons to Latin America, where the world's largest number of Catholics reside, has become particularly clear. When compared with the 8 percent of beatifieds from 1900 to 2012, the Latin American share was 10.3 percent under John Paul II, 10.9 percent under Benedict XVI, and 15.2 percent under Francis I (through 2017).

Latin America has increasingly become the front line for competition between Catholicism and Protestantism. The intensity of this competition is not surprising because Latin America has the largest share of Catholics in the world (39 percent in 2010 according to the Pew Research Center 2013). Pope John Paul II vividly referred to Protestant groups in his 1992 address to the Latin American episcopate as "rapacious wolves" who were "luring Latin American Catholics away from the Church of Rome." To dramatize his point, he added, "Huge sums of money were being spent on evangelical proselytizing campaigns which were aimed specifically at Catholics." Pope John Paul II went on to underscore that Latin America historically is a Catholic continent and that Protestants were intentionally seeking to destroy the faith, Catholicism, which defines and unifies the countries of Latin America. The pope recommended a return to "popular religiosity ... which can serve ... as an antidote against the sects" (Catholic Church 1992, p. 12).

The Catholic Church's concern with Protestant competition in Latin America goes back to the independence of the former Spanish colonies (1810–1824). At that time, when the newly independent governments terminated official relations with the Vatican, Protestants entered the countries and were openly evangelizing. Some nascent governments welcomed missionaries as they established schools and hospitals and served the indigenous populations. Immigration policies were introduced encouraging foreign non-Catholics to settle and start commercial as well as agricultural enterprises.

Pope Pius VII (in office from 1800 to 1823) was in a delicate position with Spain and King Ferdinand VII and could not readily recognize the governments of the newly independent Latin American countries. Yet, the longer the Vatican waited to establish formal relations with what remained of Church hierarchy, the weaker its position became. Cardinal Ercole Consalvi warned Pope Leo XII that Latin America would be lost to Rome, filled with "Methodists, Presbyterians and even sun worshippers." The Vatican could not wait for the Spanish monarch's permission to fill long-vacant ecclesiastical positions (Frederick Nielsen 1906, p. 10; J. Lloyd Mecham 1966, p. 76). Pope Leo XII, in an encyclical of May 5, 1824, reasserted the anti-Protestant position laid out in the Council of Trent (1545–1563) by condemning religious tolerance, freedom of conscience to choose one's religious beliefs, liberty to join "the sect that pleases him," and Protestant Bible societies promoting vernacular translations of scripture.[2]

In March 1829, Pope Pius VIII began his administration with an encyclical that condemned the Protestant Bible societies (Nielsen 1906, pp. 43–44). On May 8, 1844, Pope Gregory XVI issued a vehemently worded encyclical attacking the work of Protestant Bible societies and the ecumenical Evangelical Alliance, which Protestants had recently formed in England. The Vatican's official position was that these Protestant organizations were seeking to undermine the dominant position of the Catholic Church by advocating religious tolerance through political reform that favored Protestant entry (p. 78).

In 1864, Pope Pius IX issued an encyclical with an appended Syllabus of Errors, condemning various current trends, among them political liberalism and religious tolerance. This move to prohibit freedom of thought and expression served only to further alienate the Church from the majority of European and Latin American elites who were supporting newly created secular governments that were expanding civil liberties and political rights.

In May 1897, Pope Leo XIII issued the encyclical *Divinum Illud Munus* ("On the Holy Spirit") that promoted a charismatic movement within the Catholic Church. This move came after decades in which the Holiness and more recent pentecostal movements in the United States sent missionaries to China, India, and Latin America. The Vatican's concern with increasing Protestant competition might have been a factor in Pope Leo XIII's call for a charismatic movement as a counter-response.

Saint Making and Religious Competition

As already mentioned, our detailed analysis focuses on the role of saint making as a method that the Catholic Church employs to combat competition from Protestantism. We speculate that the Vatican promoted saints particularly as a way to raise collective identity through participation in rituals. The importance of rituals was stressed by the sociologist Émile Durkheim. As we discussed in our study of the club model in Chapter 6, Durkheim ([1915] 2008, p. 10) viewed religion as a social phenomenon: "Religious representations are collective representations which express collective realities; the rites are a manner of acting which take rise in the midst of the assembled groups and which are destined to excite, maintain or recreate mental states in these groups." Steven Pfaff (2013, pp. 197–200) argues that a group's joint veneration of saints fits within Durkheim's framework. In this case, communal acts of devotion to saints reinvigorate the faithful through shared collective emotional and psychological experiences.

Experimental anthropologist Dimitris Xygalatas (2012), in his research on extreme religious rituals, sought to physically measure the "state of effervescence" posited by Durkheim ([1915] 2008, p. 422). The annual fire walking ritual of the Spanish village of San Pedro Manrique involves devotees carrying someone on their back as they walk barefoot across hot coals. Using heart-rate monitors, Xygalatas found a synchronicity in heart rates among participating devotees, their passengers, and the observers of extreme religious rituals. His research demonstrates that even the observers of a religious ritual gain spiritual and psychological benefits similar to those participating.

THE PROCESS OF BECOMING A SAINT

Our main study applies to regular saints, known as confessors—individuals who lived a heroic life of virtue and may have suffered persecution of some form for their faith but were not put to death. Thus, we do not consider in detail martyrs, who were persecuted and killed in the cause of the Church and were often chosen in large numbers. For example, shortly after becoming pope in 2013, Francis I canonized the 813 martyrs of Otranto who were executed in 1480 following an Ottoman siege of their southern Italian city.

An important feature of sainthood is that it entails an often lengthy process that culminates in two main stages: first, designation as a blessed person (beatification) and, second, promotion to the status of a saint (canonization). Our main data on persons named as beatifieds and saints cover the period since 1588, when official Vatican records began.[3] Less complete information is available back to 1234, after which designation as a saint formally required papal approval and could not reflect merely local popularity.

Here is a brief history of the selection procedures. Beatification requires the posthumous performance of a miracle—one since John Paul II's 1983 reforms, two or more before that. Beatification is almost always required for the second stage, canonization, which requires another, post-beatification miracle (two additional miracles before the 1983 reforms). In contrast to confessors, martyrs need no miracles to be beatified.

The first recognized papal canonization occurred in 993 when Pope John XV canonized Ulric of Augsburg a mere twenty years after Ulric's death. In contrast, the average time between death and canonization since 1590 has been almost two hundred years. The process of canonization gradually became formalized up to the twelfth century. In 1234, Pope Gregory IX declared the exclusive authority of the Holy See to bestow the title of "saint." However, this decree did not deter local bishops from conferring beatifications, thereby creating a clear distinction between "saint" and "beatified."

Pope Sixtus V's creation of the Congregation of Rites in 1588 formalized the saint-making process and concentrated authority within the Holy See. The congregation was assigned authority over canonization, particularly with regard to verifying miracles and virtues. For the first time the process included medical examiners, who were charged with verifying that a person had existed (by examining the remains) and with confirming the posthumous miracles (for example, by examining the persons who claimed to be cured of disease). Sixtus V also purged the Calendar of Saints of persons with questionable credentials.

An important development in 1917 was the collection of canonical materials into a single authoritative reference known as the Pio-Benedictine Code (named for Pope Pius X, 1903–1914, and Pope Benedict XV, 1914–1922). For our purposes, the Pio-Benedictine Code is important because it laid out clearly the rules for beatification and canonization. Canon 1999 stipulates that only the pope has the authority to canonize, that the Congregation of Rites is charged with overseeing the process, and that local ecclesiastical authorities must follow canon law. Canons 2038 and 2039 stipulate that the process of naming blessed persons should typically be initiated by local Catholic authorities, and Canon 2101 reaffirms the long-held condition that fifty years must elapse after a person's death before a petition can be made.

In 1969, Pope Paul VI created the Congregation for the Causes of Saints, which replaced the Congregation of Rites. Pope John Paul II decentralized the process in 1983, while strengthening the Vatican's ability to review cases by creating the College of Relators. A relator is a high-ranking member of the Roman Curia who supervises the preparation of materials presented to the Congregation for the Causes of Saints. John Paul II also eliminated the Devil's Advocate, who had for centuries assumed the role of posing objections to proposed blessed persons.

In the current structure, the bishop and other church authorities from the location of a candidate's death oversee the collection of evidentiary materials in the first phase of the beatification process. After a five-year waiting period following the death of the candidate, a formal petition can be submitted to Rome to open the case for beatification. (The fifty-year waiting period for beatification has been dropped.) Upon Rome's approval, the local diocese appoints a postulator, who gathers evidentiary materials—writings by the candidate, testimonials from eyewitnesses, and secondhand accounts. The body of the candidate is exhumed and examined to ensure that the person existed. When the collection of evidence is complete, the report is sent to Rome to a relator, who reviews the report and appoints a medical expert to conduct an independent inquiry into the claimed miracles. The relator oversees the report, which is submitted to the Congregation for the Causes of Saints, consisting of twenty-five cardinals and bishops. If the candidate is deemed by the congregation to have lived a virtuous life according to Catholic theology, the candidate receives the title "venerable," the current status of Pope Pius XII. To be beatified, the candidate must be verified to have performed a miracle. This verification earns the candidate the title "blessed" as a beatified, the status accorded to Pope John Paul II in 2011. A second post-beatification miracle must be performed and verified before the candidate can be canonized as a saint. This process was completed for John Paul II and Pope John XXIII in April 2014.

TESTING OUR HYPOTHESES ABOUT SAINT MAKING

Our study isolates the principal determinants of numbers of persons beatified and canonized by each of the thirty-eight popes with terms begun since 1590 and completed by 2013. This sample includes blessed persons named through the end of the term of Pope Benedict XVI, thus not including Francis I. We studied choices across seven world regions: Italy, other Western Europe, Eastern Europe, Latin America, North America, Asia, and Africa.[4]

Table 7.1 gives basic facts from 1590 to 2012 (prior to the installation of Pope Francis I) about popes and their choices of blessed persons. The lengths of popes' terms varied from a few weeks (Urban VII in 1590 and John Paul I in 1978) to over twenty-five years (Pius IX, 1846–1878; John Paul II, 1978–2005; and Leo XIII, 1878–1903).

Figure 7.2 shows the regional patterns in choices of beatifieds (with a similar pattern applying to persons canonized). The graph makes clear the long-term dominance of Italy and other Western Europe but also shows the recent rise in representation for Latin America, Eastern Europe, North America, Asia, and Africa.

We have some information on socioeconomic characteristics of blessed persons. One trend is that the early emphasis on males (77 percent of those chosen as beatifieds from 1590 to 1899) has shifted to gender equality (males were 51 percent since 1900). The percentage with some formal education rose from 75 percent for 1590–1899 to 85 percent since 1900. The percentage coming from urban areas was roughly stable—78 percent for 1590–1899 and 74 percent since 1900.

Another trend is an increase in the share of beatified persons with lay status—from 35 percent for 1590–1899 to 48 percent since 1900. This shift, which began by the early twentieth century, relates to the dramatic decline since the mid-1960s in men and women joining religious orders and in men becoming candidates for the priesthood. Some scholars explain this decline as a response to Vatican II (1962–1965), which placed lay religious dedication on the same level as religious vocation.[5] However, the shift toward more blessed persons with lay status began well before Vatican II.

TABLE 7.1. Popes' Terms from 1590 to 2013

ID	Name	Start	End	Tenure (years)	Beatified			Canonized	
					Stock	Duration	Flow	Stock	Flow
226	Urban VII	1590	1590	0.04	4	103	0	35	0
227	Gregory XIV	1590	1591	0.87	4	103	0	35	0
228	Innocent IX	1591	1591	0.17	4	104	0	35	0
229	Clement VIII	1592	1605	13.09	4	104	3	35	2
230	Leo XI	1605	1605	0.07	7	70	0	37	0
231	Paul V	1605	1621	15.72	7	70	13	37	2
232	Gregory XV	1621	1623	2.41	20	36	2	39	5
233	Urban VIII	1623	1644	20.99	17	43	8	44	2
234	Innocent X	1644	1655	10.32	24	40	3	46	0
235	Alexander VII	1655	1667	12.13	27	46	1	46	2
236	Clement IX	1667	1669	2.47	26	58	1	48	2
237	Clement X	1670	1676	6.24	25	59	5	50	5
238	Innocent XI	1676	1689	12.90	25	58	3	55	0
239	Alexander VIII	1689	1691	1.32	28	64	1	55	5
240	Innocent XII	1691	1700	9.22	24	60	0	60	0
241	Clement XI	1700	1721	20.31	24	69	2	60	4
242	Innocent XIII	1721	1724	2.83	22	82	0	64	0
243	Benedict XIII	1724	1730	5.74	22	85	3	64	9
244	Clement XII	1730	1740	9.58	16	66	4	73	4

245	Benedict XIV	1740	1758	17.69	16	66	8	77	4
246	Clement XIII	1758	1769	10.59	20	66	4	81	6
247	Clement XIV	1769	1774	5.32	18	67	2	87	0
248	Pius VI	1775	1799	24.53	20	66	19	87	0
249	Pius VII	1800	1823	23.45	39	52	7	87	4
250	Leo XII	1823	1829	5.38	41	62	5	92	0
251	Pius VIII	1829	1830	1.67	46	61	0	92	0
252	Gregory XVI	1831	1846	15.34	46	62	4	92	5
253	Pius IX	1846	1878	31.67	45	76	16	97	5
254	Leo XIII	1878	1903	25.42	55	88	23	102	11
255	Pius X	1903	1914	11.05	68	80	11	113	4
256	Benedict XV	1914	1922	7.39	75	80	4	117	3
257	Pius XI	1922	1939	17.02	76	86	30	120	24
258	Pius XII	1939	1958	19.62	83	82	38	143	30
259	John XXIII	1958	1963	4.60	92	80	6	173	10
260	Paul VI	1963	1978	15.14	88	81	33	183	16
261	John Paul I	1978	1978	0.09	105	75	0	199	0
262	John Paul II	1978	2005	26.52	105	75	319	199	80
263	Benedict XVI	2005	2013	7.87	344	28	92	279	42
—	Francis I	2013	—	—	399	30	—	321	—

Note: For **beatified**, stock is the number outstanding (not yet canonized) at the start of each pope's term, duration is the mean number of years at the start of each pope's term that the beatifieds have been waiting for promotion, and flow is the number chosen by each pope. For **canonized**, stock is the cumulative number chosen up to the start of each pope's term and flow is the number chosen by each pope.

From Barro, Robert J., and Rachel M. McCleary. "Saints Marching In, 1590–2012," *Economica* 83 (July 2016), 385–415. John Wiley and Sons.

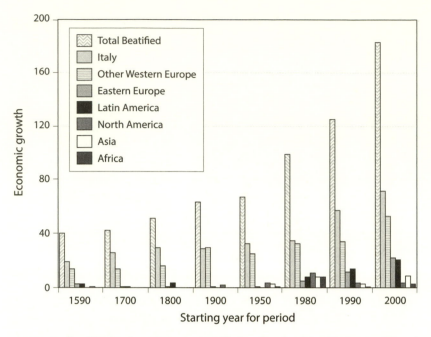

FIGURE 7.2. Beatifications by region over time. The location of each beatified person is based on the person's location at time of death (typically also the place in which the person was primarily located while in the service of the Church). From Barro, Robert J., and McCleary, Rachel M. "Saints Marching In, 1590–2012," *Economica* (2016), John Wiley and Sons.

The total number of beatified persons (non-martyrs) selected from 1590 to 2012 was 670 (see Table 7.1). A remarkable fact is that John Paul II picked 319 of these, while Benedict XVI picked 92—therefore, the two immediate predecessors to Francis I accounted for 61 percent of all the beatifieds chosen since 1590. For saints, 286 were chosen since 1590, with 122 or 43 percent coming from these two recent popes.

Our research examined in detail the patterns shown in Table 7.1 and Figure 7.2. This analysis took account of the Catholic population of each region at each date, along with other variables, including the length of a pope's term and his age when entering office. Twice as many Catholics in a region leads, other things the same, to roughly twice as many beatifieds chosen. Similarly, a doubling of a pope's term implies roughly twice as many blessed persons chosen.

Older popes tend to choose blessed persons more rapidly (perhaps to be sure of picking a desired number before dying).

One strong pattern is the discrimination in choices of blessed persons in favor of Italy, followed by other Western Europe, Eastern Europe, and the other regions (where we classified people in terms of residence at death). Other things the same, the number of blessed persons from Italy was multiplied by 4 compared with other Western Europe, 8 with Eastern Europe, 19 with North America, 33 with Latin America, 37 with Asia, and 50 with Africa. Therefore, an ending of geographical discrimination would require a truly momentous shift in the naming of blessed persons away from Europe and toward the rest of the world.

We noted before the unprecedented pace of beatification and canonization under John Paul II and Benedict XVI. Our research found that John Paul II was, indeed, extraordinary in terms of persons beatified and canonized. Other things the same (including Catholic populations), he chose seven times as many beatified persons per year and four times as many canonized persons per year, compared with the actions of previous popes. These findings accord with the fears expressed by Lawrence Cunningham (2005, pp. 121–122): "The prodigal use of this process [making saints] has been the subject of some wonder and criticism, both in Rome and in other parts of the church. The criticism comes mainly from those (including some in the Roman curia) who think both that the process is too hasty and that the multiplication of new saints cheapens the whole notion of those who are in the canon of the saints."

In contrast, we found that Benedict XVI was less of an outlier for beatified persons (choosing four times as many per year compared with popes prior to John Paul II) and within the norm for canonizations. The forty-two persons canonized during Benedict's papacy was high in historical perspective mainly because of the extraordinary rise in the number of candidates—persons already beatified— due to the large number of blessed persons selected by John Paul II.

Our main economic hypothesis concerns the Catholic Church's use of saint making as a device to compete with Protestants. To check this idea, we looked at effects on beatifications and canonizations from the extent of competition between Catholics and Protestants. We constructed a measure of this competition for each country and date. Our measure is highest when adherence rates to the two religions are similar and when adherence to other religions (Orthodox, Islam, Buddhist, etc.) is minor. Gauged this way, Latin America and Africa are the regions where Catholic-Protestant competition expanded sharply in the twentieth century because of the dramatic growth of evangelicals.

Our analysis verifies that heightened competition between Catholics and Protestants induces popes to name more blessed persons. This effect was particularly important since the early 1900s and especially in Latin America. This influence was important enough to raise the number chosen as beatifieds by as much as 50 percent in some cases. Our previously mentioned Hermano Pedro of Antigua, Guatemala, was one of the blessed persons likely chosen with an eye on competition with Protestantism.

In principle, the Catholic Church could also be using saint making to compete against religions other than Protestantism. We looked particularly at the Orthodox Church, which separated from Catholicism in the Great Schism of 1054, long before the Reformation of 1517. Our analysis found no effect on saint making from Catholic-Orthodox competition. A likely explanation is that the Catholic and Orthodox churches came to an understanding long ago not to interfere with the relationship of each church to its own members. In addition, it is hard to isolate effects from Catholic-Orthodox competition because, in contrast to Catholic-Protestant, there is little within-country overlap between Catholic and Orthodox populations—only in Eastern Europe to a significant extent.

In addition to competing with other religions, the Catholic Church became concerned in the twentieth century with the rise of no religion, an aspect of secularization that we emphasized in Chapter 2. In this case, raising enthusiasm among Catholics—perhaps through saint making—might stave off some of the departures to no religion (apostasy). That is, we can think of the Catholic Church as competing on two sides: one with Protestantism (or other religions) and the other with secularization.

To measure competition with no religion, we started by examining the fraction of each country's population classified as no religion (comprising atheists and agnostics). Many countries experienced sharp growth in this category during the twentieth century; for example, the fraction with no religion in Italy rose from 0.2 percent in 1900 to 16.5 percent in 2010, while that in Germany increased from 0.3 percent to 23.2 percent. We multiplied these increases in no-religion fractions by the Catholic share of the population in 1900 (99.7 percent for Italy, 35.6 percent for Germany). The resulting numbers gauge competition with secularization in the sense of measuring the fraction of the population that might have been persuadable (perhaps through saint making) to remain as Catholic. A key finding is that this indicator of competition with secularization rose mainly in the twentieth century and especially in Western and Eastern Europe.

Our analysis finds that greater competition with secularization tends to raise saint making. This effect was particularly important during the twentieth century and especially in Western Europe. That is, we think that the shift of persons from Catholicism to no religion in Western Europe would have been even more pronounced if not for the Catholic Church's saint-making response to the increasing propensity of Western Europeans to opt for no religion.

An interesting case not captured by our detailed analysis is the United Kingdom. Because the Catholic share of the UK population has not been high (6.3 percent in 1900 and 9.0 percent in 2010), our measures of Catholic competition with Protestantism or no religion have also not been high. The dominant adherence in the United Kingdom is to the Anglican Church (Church of England), which derives from King Henry VIII's ouster of the Catholic Church in 1534. In many theological respects, the Anglican Church remains similar to the Catholic Church. This closeness may explain the beatification of the (Catholic) English Cardinal John Henry Newman (1801–1890) by Benedict XVI in 2010. A year before Newman's beatification, Benedict XVI issued an invitation to discontented Church of England members and clergy to join the Catholic Church. The Vatican set up a structure whereby Anglicans, including married priests, could practice Catholicism while maintaining much of their own identity and liturgy. Moreover, Newman's beatification occurred at a time of a potentially serious schism in the Anglican Church over the ordination of female and homosexual priests. Thus, this particular beatification may reflect a special form of competition —the Catholic Church seeking converts from Anglicanism.

Our sample, which starts in 1590, contains part of the period of religious warfare in Western Europe from the Protestant Reformation in 1517 until the end of the Thirty Years' War with the Peace of Westphalia in 1648. These military conflicts suggest that competition between the Catholic and Protestant religions would be especially fierce in the pre-Westphalia period. Our empirical results accord with this idea because the naming of blessed persons turned out to be higher pre-1648 than post-1648. Quantitatively, we found that (other things equal) the number of beatifications pre-1648 was twice as high per year and the number of canonizations three times as high per year, compared to post-1648.

We already noted that Francis I's two predecessor popes— particularly John Paul II—accelerated the process for choosing blessed persons. Another change, likely related, is the tendency to name previous popes as blessed persons. From 1590 to 1977 (before John Paul II took office), only two popes were canonized—Pius V in 1712 and Pius X in 1954—and one more beatified—Innocent XI in 1956. In contrast, recent times saw beatifications of Pius IX and John XXIII (the great reformer of Vatican II) in 2000, John Paul II in 2011, and Paul VI in 2014. There were also remarkably rapid canonizations of John XXIII and John Paul II in 2014. Moreover, other popes are currently under active consideration for beatification, including Pius XII (controversial because of his role during World War II) and John Paul I (who served as pope for only about one month).

Blessed persons have been either confessors—the focus of our analysis—or martyrs, who were put to death because of their Catholic beliefs. Pope Francis I seems to be shifting the focus toward martyrs as a dramatic way to remind Catholics of their original faith. According to Francis I, martyrdom is the ultimate testimony, inspiring believers to witness their faith (Ann Schneible 2015). This purpose of Catholic martyrdom is similar to the role of martyrdom in Islam (David Cook 2007, p. 170). Martyrs are instrumental in strengthening the commitment of believers to the faith by high-lighting the extreme devotion represented by martyrdom. To return to Xygalatas's (2012) research on extreme religious rituals, martyr-dom is an extreme religious act, the giving of one's life for one's faith. This act sets before the faithful a spiritual height to be admired and spiritually, not physically, to be emulated. Martyrdom engenders in believers the shared "effervescence" of being Catholic, a mech-anism for bolstering their faith when confronted by proselytizing Protestants.

As a further innovation, Francis I, in his July 2017 Apostolic Let-ter, created a new category of blessed person called "offering of life" (*oblatio vitae*). This category allows for beatification of persons who made an "offering of their life" that led to their death, even if they did not die as traditional martyrs because of hatred of their faith (*odium fidei*). The new category requires "the exercise, at least in *ordinary degree* [not heroic], of the Christian virtues before the subject's offering of his or her life," and a miracle (unlike martyrs, who are beatified without a miracle). In creating this new category, Francis I made legitimate a gray area that Pope John Paul II had unofficially called "martyr of charity."

As an example of the new category, Archbishop Oscar Romero of El Salvador was assassinated in 1980 by a right-wing death squad. Canon law scholars and several Latin American cardinals argued against his beatification because his death was instigated primarily by his politics rather than by his Catholic faith. Romero's murder-ers were not acting out of odium fidei but rather were seeking to eliminate a priest who held leftist political views, was openly op-posed to the regime in power, and was popular with the people. Therefore, according to many within the Vatican, the standard cri-terion for martyrdom was not met. Nevertheless, Francis I in 2015 placed Romero under the category of "martyr of charity"—an unofficial category at the time—with Romero's beatification taking place in May 2015.

Many Catholic scholars and theologians believe the new category of oblatio vitae will increase the number of qualified candidates for beatification and, in particular, allow a pope to advance a political ideology of what constitutes an exemplary Catholic. More specifically, some conservative Catholics are concerned that Francis I will use the new category to beatify politically left-leaning Christians and liberation-theology proponents, such as Oscar Romero, who died during the armed conflicts in Latin America. Thus, a left-wing agenda seems to underlie this recent expansion of who can be chosen to be a blessed person.

One way to look at the dramatic growth in overall numbers of beatifieds and saints and the relaxation of requirements for beatification is that they represent a cheapening of the currency with regard to the value placed on sainthood. As already mentioned, Cunningham (2005, pp. 121–122) ascribed this view of recent saint-making activity to some members of the Catholic Church hierarchy. We, however, do not share this view. Our assessment is that the increased numbers and geographical spread of persons named as blessed and the targeting of popular ex-popes are clever innovations aimed at raising the enthusiasm of Catholics. The Catholic Church—the world's longest-lasting corporate enterprise—has been trying hard, partly through saint making, to maintain its powerful worldwide position by competing more effectively against evangelical Protestantism, particularly in Latin America. As suggested at the outset, this perspective accords with the high level of enthusiasm and devotion shown by pilgrims from all over the world at Hermano Pedro's tomb in Guatemala.

Cheapening Saints or Creating Catholic Effervescence?

We focused on saint making as a strategic device used by the Catholic Church to compete on one side against the growing threat from conversions into Protestant evangelicalism and on the other side against the increasing tendency of Catholics to move into no religion. The first form of competition became particularly important in Latin America and Africa in the twentieth century, and the second mattered especially in Western Europe also in the twentieth century. We argue that the Church's responses feature an increased trend toward globalization of the naming of blessed persons, particularly toward Latin America and away from the traditional focus on Italy and the rest of Western Europe.

Our study of beatifications and canonizations (non-martyrs) went back to the codification of the process in 1588. We found that, other things equal, twice as many Catholics in a region led to twice as many blessed persons and that doubling of a pope's tenure in office also led to twice as many being named. There was striking discrimination by region, with an ordering of Italy, other Western Europe, Eastern Europe, North America, Latin America, Asia, and Africa. The growing competition in the twentieth century with Protestant evangelicals and with no religion offset some of this traditional regional pattern.

We found that Pope John Paul II was a remarkable outlier, having beatified 319 of the 670 persons chosen as confessors from 1590 to 2012. Benedict XVI and Francis I have continued a high pace of beatification, but not as high as John Paul II. And much of the high numbers of canonizations under these last two popes can be explained as a response to the large number of candidates for sainthood (persons already beatified) provided by John Paul II.

The heightened tendency to beatify popular previous popes—including the recent elevations of John XXIII and John Paul II—is another way in which the Catholic Church has sought to raise the enthusiasm of its adherents. Some observers decry this process, as well as the growth in overall numbers of newly named blessed persons, as effectively a cheapening of the currency in the sense of lowering the value attached to sainthood. However, we disagree and instead view the recent developments as clever strategic devices for maintaining the powerful position of the Catholic Church.

One gap in our analysis is that we have not documented the ways in which the Catholic Church's strategic expansions of saint making have succeeded or not. We would like systematic evidence that the naming of saints actually makes adherents more enthusiastic about Catholicism and reduces movements toward alternative religions— especially Protestant evangelicalism—and toward no religion.

One study in this spirit is by the sociologist Steven Pfaff (2013). He analyzed the tendency of German cities to shift from 1523 to 1545, after the Reformation, away from Catholicism and toward the new Protestant faith. He found (in his Table 3) that the probability of adopting Protestantism, rather than remaining exclusively Catholic or choosing a bi-confessional setup, was significantly negatively related to the number of saints' shrines per capita that were established up to 1530. Moreover, the explanatory role of this shrines variable seemed to indicate a special role for saints because another measure of a city's religious institutions—the number of monasteries per person in 1500—had no explanatory power for the adoption of Protestantism. These findings from the post-Reformation period fit with our hypothesis that the increased use of saint making helps the Catholic Church to sustain its membership.

Another possibility is to merge our data on blessed persons with a data set developed by Jonathan Shultz. His data cover the establishment of bishoprics in Europe from the beginning of the sixth century until 1500, when a region/country was incorporated into the Medieval Catholic Church's administration (Shultz et al. 2018). Given the central role of bishops in the beatification of local saints, we could look at the spread of the cult of saints during the same time period as the spread of bishoprics. How quickly were beatifications occurring after a bishopric was established? To what degree did bishops co-opt local cults and regional observances of relics and statues? And for what purpose were they integrated into the Catholic liturgy and faith?

A further idea is to apply the framework on saints to the Catholic Church's selection of cardinals. For this purpose, researchers can use the remarkable data set on cardinals constructed by Salvador Miranda (2018). This data set gives names and characteristics, including residence at birth, of the 4,371 cardinals chosen from

494 to 2017. Thus, these data cover a much longer period and comprise many more designees compared to the sample of non-martyr blessed persons. One idea would be to study the changing geographical composition of the cardinals. As a minor but concrete example of possible effects, Richard Ault, Robert Ekelund, and Robert Tollison (1987) argue from the standpoint of political economy that a shift in the mix of cardinals toward regions, such as the Americas, that are more concentrated in production of beef compared to fish helps to explain the Catholic Church's shift in 1966 away from the requirement of eating fish on Fridays.[6]

It would be important to extend our analysis of choices of confessors to the selection of martyrs. The data on martyrs are available over the long term, but a challenge is how to deal with the large numbers often chosen simultaneously as a single group. How do we compare eight hundred martyrs selected together with the choice of a single confessor? And how do we take account of the different requirements for the two categories of blessed persons—martyrs do not need a miracle to be beatified but must have died through persecution based on their relation to the Church.

As with Salvadoran Archbishop Oscar Romero, politics can complicate the process of choosing martyrs. A famous case is Joan of Arc. Depending on your perspective, she was either a martyr (French Catholic) or a heretical political prisoner believed to be a witch (English). If we made the extension of our data to encompass martyrs, we could also examine in detail the choices being made currently by Pope Francis I. As mentioned, our casual inspection suggested increased weight being put on martyrs. However, it would be informative to examine this conjecture from the perspective of a detailed historical comparison.

Finally, other religions, such as Orthodox, Islam, Hinduism, and Buddhism, have categories of sainthood and martyrdom. The procedures for choosing saints in these religions appear to be less clear-cut than those applying in Catholicism, but there do exist lists of persons generally recognized as saints. Creating data sets on saints and martyrs for other religions would allow researchers to assess the characteristics that qualify individuals for sainthood and martyrdom in these religions. We could also examine, as we did for the Catholic Church, whether the selection of blessed persons is sensitive to inter-religion competition and whether these selections matter for future levels of this competition.

8

The Wealth of Religions

Some years ago, we gave a series of lectures on religion and political economy at Seoul National University in South Korea. South Korea has seen dramatic growth over recent decades in religiosity in the form of Protestant evangelicalism. In the first lecture, a young Korean man sitting in the first row smiled and pointed to an enormous silver cross that he was proudly wearing. No doubt he thought that we were kindred spirits, having brought the enlightenment of Christianity to the traditionally secular area of political economy. But our analytical approach ended up disappointing him.

We think that the young man was seeking a normative approach, whereby we would argue that a particular religious doctrine (likely evangelical Protestantism) was intrinsically correct and ought to have greater influence over social choices than it currently enjoys. Instead, we were pursuing what John Neville Keynes (1890, pp. 34–35, 46) and Milton Friedman (1953, pp. 3–7) described as "positive science" or, more specifically, "positive economics."[1]

According to Friedman (p. 4), "Positive economics is in principle independent of any particular ethical position or normative judgments.... It deals with what is, not with what ought to be. Its task is to ... make correct predictions about the consequences of any change in circumstances.... Positive economics is, or can be, an objective science." In contrast, Keynes (p. 34) says, "A normative ... science ... [is] a body of systematized knowledge relating to criteria of what ought to be, and concerned therefore with the ideal as distinguished from the actual." But Friedman (p. 5) closed the circle by noting, "Normative economics ... cannot be independent of positive economics. Any policy conclusion necessarily rests on a prediction about the consequences of doing one thing rather than another, a prediction that must be based ... on positive economics."

In carrying out our positive analysis of religion and its interplay with political economy, we do concern ourselves with religious theology. Specifically, we think that religious beliefs held by adherents are central to making positive predictions about how religion influences economic development and other aspects of society. In our framework, believing matters particularly when considered in relation to belonging, which we gauge by participation in formal religious services and other measures of the resources used by the religion sector. That is, we put a lot of weight on believing and belonging.

Believing and Belonging

Our view is that the special contribution of religion to society derives from religious beliefs. Religion is sui generis, featuring conceptions of salvation, damnation, and afterlife. These non-verifiable supernatural beliefs can be great motivators of behavior in this world. As argued by Max Weber ([1904–1905] 1930), the Protestant Reformation stressed religious beliefs that served as the foundation for individual traits such as work ethic, thrift, and honesty. These traits likely supported the Industrial Revolution in Western Europe in the 1700s and, thereby, helped to spur the success of modern capitalism.

According to Weber (p. 72), the reliance of wealth accumulation and capitalism on religious principles had ended sometime before his own lifetime, which began in 1864: "Modern capitalism has become dominant and has become emancipated from its old supports." Nevertheless, as discussed in Chapters 2 and 3, we investigated Weber's ideas on the spirit of capitalism with modern data. We concluded that religious beliefs—notably in hell and heaven—continue to be important drivers of economic growth. More specifically, we found that believing relative to belonging (gauged by attendance at formal religious services) was an important determinant of growth. We guess it is fair to say that we have become more Weberian than Weber himself, since he would have not have anticipated these kinds of results for data covering the twentieth and twenty-first centuries.

If it is believing relative to belonging that promotes economic growth, the belonging part is productive only if its contribution to beliefs more than offsets its direct use of resources (including time spent on religious activities and personal prayer and money expended on religious buildings and personnel). The social-capital aspects of religion—communal services, rituals, educational classes—are productive in this framework only to the extent that they instill religious beliefs. For given beliefs, our results imply that more resources spent on formal religion signal that the religion sector is less productive. Specifically, our findings conflict with the view that religion is one way among many to build social capital, with this social capital then being the key determinant of economic development.

In Chapter 6, we focused on the applications of the club model to the economics of religion. This model explains how religious groups can use costly admission requirements—sacrifice and stigma—to form a dedicated membership. This approach helps to understand unusual religious cults and standard religious denominations. It also provides insights about nonreligious organizations, including those that support terrorism. Therefore, the club model is an important conceptual advance. Nevertheless, this model fits into our thinking about religion and political economy only by helping to understand the belonging part of the believing-versus-belonging paradigm. We have to look elsewhere to evaluate Max Weber's thesis that the Protestant ethic spurred economic growth through religious beliefs that enhanced key character traits such as work ethic and thrift.

We also assessed the idea, related to Martin Luther's stress on individual reading of the Bible, that Protestantism could influence economic development by promoting education and human capital. The research by Becker and Woessmann (2009) for nineteenth-century Prussia and by Boppart et al. (2014) for nineteenth-century Switzerland verified this channel of effects. However, these findings do not rule out Weber's Protestant ethic, which emphasizes work ethic. Support for the Weberian hypothesis comes from Basten and Betz (2013) and Spenkuch (2017), who found from modern data for Switzerland and Germany, respectively, that part of Protestantism's favorable effect on economic outcomes involved a positive linkage between Protestantism and work ethic.

In future research, it would be good to separate further religiosity's effects on character traits such as work effort and thrift from those involving education. It might work to gauge the character traits by using survey questions from the World Values Survey, which asks, first, how important is work in one's life and, second, whether hard work and thrift should be included in a list of qualities that children can be encouraged to learn at home. These survey data can be linked to individual religious affiliation and to outcomes on education and income.

We also think it worthwhile to expand existing analyses of the economic influences of religion-based laws and regulations. In Chapters 3 and 5, we discussed economic implications of state religions and of government regulation of the religion market. In Chapter 4, we argued that economic growth in Muslim countries after the Industrial Revolution was impeded by weak legal and regulatory institutions. Problematic aspects of Islam's history include rigid inheritance laws, restrictions on credit and insurance, weak contract enforcement, and, perhaps most importantly, the lack of a legal basis for corporate structure. However, this analysis was more impressionistic than quantitative, and it would be valuable to carry out more rigorous, quantitative studies. This analysis could use Jonathan Fox's (2018) international data (available back to 1991) to gauge religion-inspired laws and regulations at the country level. Hence, this work can examine the economic consequences of religion-based laws and regulations in a broad cross-country sample.

As mentioned in Chapter 4, research on the economic implications of religion has been overly weighted toward Christianity, probably because of the great impact of Max Weber's ([1904–1905] 1930) epic work, which focused on the post-Reformation distinction between Protestantism and Catholicism. We did discuss economic effects from Islamic laws and regulations. We also touched briefly on the economic content of other religions, including Hinduism, Buddhism, and Judaism. But more research on other religions would be useful. Some questions to consider include the following: Is there anything in the idea that Hinduism and Buddhism tend to associate with economic growth that is neither too high nor too low but rather follows more of a middle path? Is there any economic consequence in Jews seeming to have lost their vision of an afterlife? Is it true that a philosophy such as Confucianism or a nonreligious moral code can be a satisfactory substitute for formal religion? And, going beyond economic growth, what are the consequences of state religion and religious regulation for religious freedom and for the maintenance more broadly of civil liberties and democracy?

Diffusion of Religion

One understudied area is the diffusion of religion over space. Historically, much of the spread of religious adherence involved the interrelated effects of conquest and trade. An example is Islam's geographical expansion from the time of Muhammad in the early 600s to the peak of the Ottoman and other Muslim empires in the late 1500s. Residents of conquered territories typically converted more or less voluntarily to Islam. Given the prominence of trade for many Muslims, the shape of the conquest and religious expansion often followed trade routes. As Bradley Skeen (2008) says, "Trade, as a profession, always held a more favored position in the Islamic world than in Europe. Trade was for many Muslims almost a necessity, since carrying small amounts of merchandise to sell along the way was a common means of financing the pilgrimage to Mecca that all Muslims had to make in their lifetime." Hence, there is reason to expect that expansions of Islamic adherence would be closely connected to historical trade patterns.

The effects of trading routes on Islamic adherence were studied in detail by Stelios Michalopoulos, Alireza Naghavi, and Giovanni Prarolo (2018). They found (Table 1) that adherence to Islam in 1900 across 127 countries in Europe, Asia, and Africa was strongly negatively related to a place's distance from the pre-600 trading network. In contrast, this trading-route distance was positively related (in their Table 5) to Christian adherence. Also important in a negative direction for Islam adherence was the distance from the historical Muslim center of Mecca, Saudi Arabia (their Table 1). This distance from Mecca is analogous to the distance from Wittenberg, the variable used by Becker and Woessmann (2009) to study the spread of Protestantism in Germany after the Reformation in the 1500s. As we noted in Chapter 3, the Wittenberg variable has a major negative effect on the fraction of the German population in the 1870s that was Protestant, rather than Catholic. Similarly, the distance-from-Mecca variable helps to explain the diffusion of Islam from its Meccan origins.

In Africa, the combined effects from conquests, colonizations, and missionary conversions led in 2000 to an adhering population that averaged 40 percent Islam, 14 percent Catholic, and 28 percent Protestant (with the remainder identified mostly as indigenous religions).[2] In the sub-Saharan part of Africa, these percentages were 29 percent Islam, 17 percent Catholic, and 34 percent Protestant, whereas in North Africa they were 92 percent Islam, 0.2 percent Catholic, and 0.7 percent Protestant.

In Western Europe and North America, Muslims have been growing in population share especially due to migration from Africa and Asia. Examples are Muslims coming to France from former French colonies in North Africa and those coming to the United Kingdom from Pakistan and India (also former colonies). Aside from migration, the rising Muslim share over time in Western Europe and North America reflects fertility rates among Muslims that are higher than those of non-Muslims.

In the Indian subcontinent, Islam spread primarily through trade in southern coastal areas with good ports (as stressed by Saumitra Jha 2013) and mainly by conquest and religious movements in interior regions.[3] Our conjecture is that where Islam spread via maritime trade and never became a "ruling religion," Muslims would be better integrated today into mainstream society as reflected in labor market and other indicators.

The southern coast of India was a part of a much larger oceanic trade network. Pre-Islam Arab maritime merchants traded along the Indian coast. After the establishment of the Abbasid Caliphate (762–1258) in Baghdad, Iraq, Muslim merchants traveled to Sumatran ports. By the ninth century, the merchants of the Muslim seaports of Basra (Iraq) and Siraf (Iran) established regular trading routes to India and Southeast Asia. Permanent Muslim trading communities settled on the Malabar Coast and in Southeast Asia, linking commercial circuits in the Arabian Sea, the Bay of Bengal, and the South China Sea. Through established commercial interactions between the Arabian Sea trading network, southern (Malabar) coast, and maritime Southeast, Islam gained adherents.

For Burma (now Myanmar), Arab, Persian, and Indian Muslim traders engaged in maritime trading along the coast, slowly integrating into local communities. A wave of Muslim immigrants from India after the 1852 British annexation of Lower Burma changed Burma's religious-ethnic-economic dynamics. This wave of immigrants gained positions in industry, transport, trade, the export and import business, and the army and police, although they never constituted more than 3 to 4 percent of the population. Whereas those of recent Indian Muslim descent sought to retain their distinctive cultural patterns, the Burmese Muslims, going back centuries, had assimilated into the dominant culture, differing from their fellow citizens of the Buddhist faith only in religion.

In places where their faith spread by conquest, Muslims today would be more marginalized. For example, Paul Brass (2010), in his discussion of the early post-independence years after the 1947 Partition of India, discusses how in the state of Uttar Pradesh police were "de-Muslimized" deliberately because Muslims were initially overrepresented in the police. The result has been severe underrepresentation subsequently of Muslims in local police forces across North India.

Another possible channel from modes of diffusion to current occupational structure is that in places where Islam arrived via trade and Muslims began as traders, Muslims tend still to be engaged in trading activity. In contrast, places where Islam arrived via conquest and new cities were settled as part of that process, Muslims tend to be administrators and artisans. After Indian independence, the administration became predominantly Hindu, while Muslim artisans remained. Hence, particularly with the rigidities created by the caste system, the original difference between Muslim traders and Muslim artisans likely continues to the present day.

Conquest in the form of colonization was central to the spread of Christianity from Europe to the Americas, Africa, and parts of Asia. For example, Latin America became predominantly Catholic following the colonizations in the 1500s by Spain and Portugal. However, as discussed in Chapter 7, competition from Protestant evangelicals leading to many religious conversions led in the twenty-first century to near balance between Catholicism and Protestantism in many Latin American countries. In North America, the dominance of Protestant and Catholic representation reflects partly colonizations by England and France and partly the religious compositions of much later waves of immigration.

We are currently carrying out research to understand the slow diffusion of Islam to Latin America. The World Religion Database (WRD) indicates that Muslim numbers in Latin America were 58,000 (0.09 percent of the population) in 1900, 230,000 (0.14 percent) in 1950, 425,000 (0.15 percent) in 1970, 1.44 million (0.27 percent) in 2000, and 1.72 million (0.27 percent) in 2015. Thus, the main growth in population share occurred from 1970 to 2000, and the level still remains well below 1 percent.

Within Latin America, the dominant place that the WRD identifies for Muslims in 2015 is Argentina (930,000 people, constituting 2.1 percent of the population). The presence of Muslims in Argentina goes back to the nineteenth century, when the country was a favored destination for Arab immigrants (Abdeluahed Akmir

2009). The role of Muslims in Argentina is particularly interesting to study because of Islam's increased visibility in the country starting in the 1990s. On the negative side are the bombings of the Israeli embassy and a Jewish community center in 1992 and 1994. Investigations of these cases, involving Hezbollah and Iran and cover-ups by Argentinean politicians, are still ongoing. On a more positive note, the King Fahd Islamic Cultural Centre—the largest mosque in Latin America—was built in Buenos Aires in 1996. This building was funded by Saudi Arabia and constructed on land provided by then president Carlos Menem (of Syrian descent, married to a practicing Muslim and himself a former Muslim). In 2011, President Cristina Kirchner pursued a more liberal approach to Argentina's Muslim minority by passing legislation to permit the wearing of hijabs in public.

Other smaller Latin American countries with substantial Muslim representation in 2015 are: Guyana (7.5 percent, 58,000 people), Suriname (5.9 percent, 86,000 people), and Trinidad and Tobago (6.4 percent, 88,000 people). Brazil in 2015 had a substantial number of Muslims (207,000), though a small share of the population (0.1 percent).

One hypothesis is that the scarcity of Muslims in Latin America reflects primarily geography. Latin America is the farthest away from Islam whether gauged by the theological center in Mecca, Saudi Arabia, or the concentrations of Muslim populations, dominated currently by Indonesia, India, Pakistan, Bangladesh, Nigeria, Egypt, Iran, and Turkey. (According to the WRD, these eight countries accounted in 2015 for 1.04 billion or 60 percent of the world's 1.72 billion Muslims.) Traveling from Muslim centers to Latin America is more difficult than, for example, traveling to Europe. This idea accords with the finding by Michalopoulos, Naghavi, and Prarolo (2018, Table 1) that the Muslim share of the population for 127 countries in Europe, Asia, and Africa is inversely related to a place's distance from Mecca.

We plan to build on the distance-to-Mecca variable to gain further insights about the small numbers of Muslims residing in Latin America. Possibilities include the absence of links to long-ago Islamic trade routes or conquests (as is also true for North America) and the lack of colonial ties to countries with heavy Muslim representation (which are important for parts of Western Europe). Another consideration is that migrants of any type tend to come when a critical mass of persons with the same ethnicity and religion are already present. Thus, a large flow of Muslim immigration to Latin America might take place at some future date once the critical mass has been reached.

Religion and Science

The relation between religion and science has long been debated. When science disproves specific religious claims, such as creation stories in sacred texts, the inerrancy and legitimacy of religion would be expected to weaken. Yet, the importance of religion does not depend on literal interpretations of the Bible or of theology more broadly. And religious beliefs and imagination can and do expand the range of meaningful questions that we hypothesize about. Why was the universe created? What is special about our planet in this universe? Questions about other intelligent life forms in the universe naturally follow from belief in supernatural entities such as angels and demons.

We agree with the scientist Carl Sagan ([1985] 2006) that scientific enquiry can enlighten religion in the sense that empirical findings disprove sacred interpretations of the universe or expose erroneous reasoning when it comes to harmful practices such as slavery. The mysteries of the transcendent will always remain with us, and we need to approach them with critical thinking, open-mindedness, and tolerance.

Thomas Aquinas ([1920] 2017, p. Q50) understood angels to be pure intellect of spiritual substance. Dionysius (1897–1899, IX, Sec. II) called them "heavenly minds." Albert Einstein (discussed in Karl Seelig 1954, pp. 261–262) held a similar view, referring to "a belief bound up with deep feeling in a superior mind that reveals itself in the world of experience, represents my conception of God." Religious beliefs in and imaginings of transcendent beings allow us to think outside the box, to conceive of possibilities beyond our own limitations. These beliefs can push the boundaries of scientific inquiry, including social-science inquiries such as ours, while at the same time being subjected to empirical testing, and, at times, being intellectually desacralized or secularized. But, of course, some types of supernatural religious beliefs are nonverifiable, not subject directly to scientific confirmation or refutation.

The secularization hypothesis states that as societies grow richer, they become less religious, gauged by beliefs and participation. In accord with this reasoning, we find that a higher level of economic development across countries and over time tends to go along with lower religiousness. However, as we argued throughout this book, secularization is not a universal truth. A sharp decline in religious participation is occurring in some societies—notably Britain, Germany, France, and Italy—but not in others—such as Poland, Ireland, the Philippines, the United States, the Muslim world, and most of sub-Saharan Africa. These examples illustrate the context-specific nature of secularization and religiosity. Furthermore, debates continue over whether secularization is the death of religion or merely one phase among many that religion goes through.

We also found that the inverse connection between economic development and religiosity did not arise because people in richer places were better educated and, hence, more scientific. There was clear evidence of negative effects on religiousness from urbanization but not from education. These patterns do not suggest a basic incompatibility between religion and knowledge or science.

Further along these lines, if we applied our findings on secularization to religious conversion, we might think that richer places would have lower conversion rates—but that is not the case. Conversion rates are roughly independent of the overall level of economic development and are positively related to education. If religion were fundamentally incompatible with knowledge and science, why would more educated persons bother to make the investments needed to change religions?

We observed that government regulation of the religion market could lower competition, thereby leading to lower quality religion products and reduced participation in formal religious services. On the other side, government intervention can raise participation by subsidizing religion providers and by banning competing secular activities, such as sports events and commerce on days of worship. Governments can also regulate competition by barring designated sects and denominations. Complementing this type of restriction are prohibitions on converting out of or into the favored religion. Often, but not always, these kinds of restrictions accompany the establishment of a state religion.

In line with the club model, religions sometimes make it costly for an individual to adopt a religion by requiring extensive religious training or even the learning of a dedicated language. Some religions make it costly to leave by shunning or treating a defector as dead and claiming that those who depart will go to hell. Other restrictions on conversion come from governments rather than religions; for example, many Muslim countries have restrictions on leaving Islam. Even when direct constraints on conversion are absent, some countries restrict proselytizing and interfaith marriage, activities that interact strongly with religious conversion. We found that the presence of these restrictions resulted in fewer religious conversions.

The role of government as a regulator of religion was discussed by Adam Smith (1791, book V, chap. I, art. III) in *The Wealth of Nations*. Religion, Smith contends, is more vibrant where there is an institutional disassociation between church and state. The absence of a state religion and heavy regulation allows for competition, thereby creating an environment for a plurality of religious faiths in society. By showing no preference for one religion over another, the state allows for an open market in which religious groups engage in rational discussion about religious beliefs, thereby promoting an atmosphere of "good temper and moderation." In these societies, the pluralistic nature of the religion market increases the likelihood of people experimenting with alternative beliefs and switching religions. In contrast, a state monopoly on religion tends to generate zealousness, the imposition of ideas on the public, and a locking-in of religious identities.

Rodney Stark and William S. Bainbridge (1987) used Smith's reasoning to build a "supply-side" model of religious participation. In their framework, greater religious pluralism—measured, for example, by the diversity of religious adherence in a country or region—tends to promote a better and more tailored religion product and leads, thereby, to greater religious participation. The larger variety of religion offerings also encourages more conversion from one faith to another.

Charles Taylor's (2010) views resemble Smith's if we think of Taylor's term "secularism" as corresponding to the religious pluralism of Smith (1791) and de Tocqueville ([1835] 2000). According to Taylor (p. 23), key features of secularism are "first, no one must be forced in the domain of religion.... This is what is often defined as religious liberty, including, of course, the freedom not to believe.... Second, there must be equality between people of different faiths ... no religious outlook ... can enjoy a privileged status, let alone be adopted as the official view of the state.... Third, all spiritual families must be heard.... Fourth ... we try as much as possible to maintain relations of harmony and comity between the supporters of different religions." Taylor then argues (p. 29) that these principles of secularism sometimes come into conflict, as in the case of France regulating the wearing of the hijab by Muslim women in public schools. Other hot-topic issues that can generate these kinds of conflicts include abortion, same-sex marriage, and polygamy.

One notable trend is that people are increasingly making changes in their religion without being constrained to remain within the faith in which they were born. The Pew Research Center (2009, 2015b) found that about half of Americans change religious affiliation at least once during their lives. This rising propensity for conversion means that loyalty to one's childhood faith is not an identity marker that precludes the experience of alternative religious practices and beliefs. Conversely, leaving one's childhood religion does not trigger social stigma and communal ostracism.

Another trend is that participation in organized religion no longer correlates fully with being religious. Specifically, there is a global movement toward the religiously unaffiliated or "none" category.

Individuals in this group seek spiritual answers outside of the traditional forms of organized religion. These nones sometimes view themselves as religious without adhering to an accepted doctrine or having a formal membership in a church, temple, or mosque. Some nones leave open the possibility of joining a religion, while others become atheists or agnostics.

Albert Einstein seems to have been a "none." He viewed the indeterminacies of quantum mechanics as conflicting with his understanding of the physical laws that governed the universe, and he viewed the underlying harmony of these laws as coming from God. Alberto Martinez (2011, p. 166) quotes Einstein as saying, "I believe in Spinoza's God who reveals himself in the orderly harmony of what exists, not in a God who concerns himself with fates and actions of human beings." Thus, Einstein was a "none" in the sense that he rejected formal religion as well as a doctrinal interpretation of God. Instead, Einstein viewed religion as a reverence for the beauty and orderliness of the universe. Spirituality as awe for that which transcends human understanding is a shared common ground for believers and nones.

We started this book by noting how audiences often wanted to know about our personal religious beliefs and attachments, perhaps because people thought that these traits would influence our investigations into the interactions between religion and political economy. Therefore, we think we should end with a quick synopsis of our religious backgrounds. Robert, an economist, is Jewish, with more of an ethnic than religious affinity. Rachel, a philosopher, is Methodist and religious. Religious identity for both of us is a matter of being born into a certain religion and, as adults, voluntarily choosing to remain within those religious traditions. We do not think that these personal religious affiliations have colored our investigations into the interactions between religion and political economy. But we will leave it to readers to decide whether we are right.

Chapter 1. Religion

1. See James T. Richardson and David G. Bromley (1983), James T. Richardson (1993), and J. Gordon Melton (2000).

2. This approach is referred to as the "church-sect" paradigm originated by Max Weber ([1904–1905] 1930) and his student, Ernst Troeltsch ([1931] 1992), and was further developed by the sociologists Charles Glock and Rodney Stark (1965).

3. See Peter Thuesen (2010, p. 229).

4. See Vera Mironova (2017), Eli Berman (2003, 2009), and Ran Abramitzky (2008, 2018).

Chapter 2. What Determines Religiousness?

1. The idea of a two-way causation between religion and economy is a central theme of the work of R. H. Tawney. For example, Tawney (1930, p. 11) says, "It is instructive to trace, with Weber, the influence of religious ideas on economic development. It is not less important to grasp the effect of the economic arrangements accepted by an age on the opinion which it holds of the province of religion."

2. See Benito Arruñada (2004) for a discussion of the role of confession.

3. The market approach to religion was elaborated upon by the sociologists Roger Finke and Rodney Stark and economist Laurence Iannaccone. See Finke and Stark (1992), Iannaccone and Finke (1993), Iannaccone and Stark (1994), and Iannaccone (1991).

4. There are several histories of Methodism, among them William Warren Sweet (1954) and, for a religion-market approach, Finke and Stark (1992).

5. More indicators of regulation of religion are provided by Fox (2018).

6. No implementations of blue laws occurred during their sample period. The states eliminating blue laws were Florida, Indiana, Iowa, Kansas, Minnesota, North Dakota, Ohio, Pennsylvania, South Carolina, South Dakota, Tennessee, Utah, Vermont, Virginia, and Washington. Eight states never had blue laws, twenty allowed for decisions at the local level, and six had unclear exceptions to blue laws.

7. For a firsthand analysis of the religion market in China, see Ian Johnson (2017). Moshe Bernstein (2017) discusses Judaism in China through the lens of the ancient Jewish Chinese community in Kaifeng.

8. For a definition of intangible cultural heritage, see UNESCO (2018).

9. China Aid is a nonprofit organization that monitors religious freedom in China. For restrictions by the Chinese government on Christians, see China Aid (2018).

10. Laurence Iannaccone (2003). Surprisingly, this innovative study has not been published and has not yet been updated.

11. However, church attendance for Ireland has since fallen sharply—down to 61 percent for the population over age sixteen by 2008.

12. The term "liminal" was coined by Chaeyoon Lim, Carol Ann MacGregor, and Robert Putnam (2010). For a discussion, see Michael Hout (2017).

13. See the interview by Kate Shellnutt, *Christianity Today*, April 7, 2017.

14. According to Rosemary Groves (1988), "Harvard has never really gotten past being called 'godless Harvard.' It is widely reported that the label dates from the abolition of compulsory chapel in 1886 when Harvard was the first college to take this action."

15. For the full development of this framework, see Rodney Stark and Roger Finke (2000) and Robert Barro, Jason Hwang, and Rachel McCleary (2010).

16. Similarly, Laurence Iannaccone (1990, pp. 301–302) found that, among converts into Catholicism in the United States, 85 percent converted before age thirty.

17. This measure also includes people with two or more conversions. According to the 1988 GSS religion module, among persons with at least one change of religion by 1988, 67 percent had one change, 25 percent two changes, and 8 percent three or more changes. However, these measures include as conversions movements to or from no religion as well as shifts within a major group, such as Protestantism.

Chapter 3. Religion and Economic Growth

1. For a detailed discussion of the relationship between religious beliefs and economic incentives in the various religions, see Rachel McCleary (2007).

2. For a discussion in the context of contemporary Muslim countries, see Sadiq Reza (2007).

3. This point reminds us of the opening scene on the bus in Alfred Hitchcock's film *The Man Who Knew Too Much*. A young American boy, Hank, is walking down the aisle of the moving bus when the vehicle suddenly lurches, sending Hank forward. As he grabs for the side of a seat, Hank's hand misses and instead grabs the veil of a seated Arab woman, yanking it off. The Arab woman screams in horror, covering her face with her hands. Her male companion rises quickly and verbally threatens Hank. A Frenchman, Louis Bernard, who is on the bus, rises to

intervene. Once the situation calms down, Hank's mother says to Bernard, "Why was he so angry? It was an accident." Bernard responds, "The Muslim religion allows for few accidents."

4. The account, often disputed, of Martin Luther nailing the announcement of his ninety-five theses on the church's north door was first written by Philipp Melanchthon, Luther's close friend.

5. For an analysis of this point, see Ian Hart (1995, pp. 43–45). Luther's argument was in two steps: (1) Each person has a calling from God to work; (2) all callings are equal in merit before God. Then Luther provided a corollary: a person should work hard at his or her calling and not seek to change his or her station.

6. Calvin's vision of a godly society in Geneva is outside the scope of this chapter. See Philip Gorski (2003).

7. Revealed theology comprises doctrinal truths revealed by God to human beings.

8. "Whoever relies not on the providence of God, so as to commit his life to its faithful guardianship, has not yet learned aright what it is to live. On the other hand, he who shall entrust the keeping of his life to God's care, will not doubt of its safety even in the midst of death. We must therefore put our life into God's hand, not only that he may keep it safely in this world, but also that he may preserve it from destruction in death itself, as Christ's own example has taught us. As David wished to have his life prolonged amidst the dangers of death, so Christ passed out of this transitory life that his soul might be saved in death." (Calvin [1563] 1845, p. 503).

9. For a discussion of the development of this core model of economic growth, see Robert Barro and Xavier Sala-i-Martin (2004, introduction).

10. The underlying statistical analysis treats participation in formal religious services and religious beliefs as potentially endogenous variables; that is, these variables might respond to variations in economic growth. To account for this possibility, the estimation uses as "instruments" for the religiosity variables the presence of a state religion around 1970, the nature of regulation of the religion market in the 1970s, a measure of pluralism of the religion market based on the dispersion of religious adherence rates, and the adherence rates to ten major religions in 1970. This procedure helps to isolate causation from the religiosity indicators to economic growth, rather than the reverse.

11. This statement applies when the two variables are considered in a proportionate sense. That is, we can think of doubling beliefs (the fraction who believe) and also doubling participation (the fraction who attend at least monthly).

12. Specifically, Becker and Woessmann used distance from Wittenberg as an instrument for Protestant population share in a cross-county regression with fraction literate as the dependent variable. The success of this distance variable in the context of the spread of Protestantism motivated Jeremiah Dittmar (2011) to carry out an analogous study of the geographical impact of the printing press, starting from Gutenberg's implementation of movable-type printing in Mainz,

Germany, around 1450. The dispersion of printing presses relative to Mainz accorded with the evolution of city population levels during the sixteenth century. Places closer to Mainz were more likely to adopt printing presses earlier and were, for that reason, more likely to have higher population growth.

Chapter 4. Islam and Economic Growth

1. The data are from the Barro-Ursúa data set, described in http://scholar.harvard.edu/barro/publications/barro-ursua-macroeconomic-data. The OECD countries included are Australia, Austria, Belgium, Canada, Denmark, Finland, France, Germany, Italy, Japan, the Netherlands, New Zealand, Norway, Portugal, Spain, Sweden, Switzerland, the United Kingdom, and the United States. This data set covers two other Muslim countries over the long term—Indonesia since 1880 and Malaysia since 1900. Indonesia's per capita GDP was 65 percent of Turkey's in 1880 and 47 percent in 2016. Malaysia's per capita GDP was 37 percent of Turkey's in 1900 but 117 percent in 2016. Since the 1960s, Malaysia has grown like East Asian miracle economies, such as Hong Kong, Singapore, South Korea, Taiwan, and Thailand.

2. For a well-regarded history of Islam, see Marshall G. Hodgson (1974).

3. From a military standpoint, the Ottoman Empire likely peaked during Suleyman's reign from 1520 to 1566 or just afterward before the military defeat in the Lepanto Sea Battle of 1571.

4. These numbers do not include persons who had failed in lotteries twice before and were, therefore, automatically given visas.

5. However, for extreme cases, such as northern Scandinavia, adjustments are made, so that each day of Ramadan does not correspond precisely to the time between sunrise and sunset.

Chapter 5. State Religion

1. Another form of government monopoly with a long history involves control over maritime and land trading routes. This form of monopoly by city-states goes back at least three thousand years. Hegemonic control of trading routes involved taxation of different kinds, prohibitions on trading of certain goods, and bans on certain trading partners as well as religionists. It is known that religions spread via ancient trade routes, for example, the Silk Road. The transmission of a religion via trade routes could influence the eventual establishment of a state religion.

2. See David Barrett (1982, pp. 800–801) and David Barrett, George Kurian, and Todd Johnson (2001, pp. 834–835).

3. An alternative classification of state religions is given from 1990 to 2008 by Fox (2018) in his *Religion and State* data set. The Fox framework puts more

weight on legal provisions than on the de facto environment and, therefore, classifies fewer countries as having an official religion. For example, in 2000, Fox has 42 of 175 or 24.0 percent of countries as having either one or multiple official religions, whereas we have 75 of 188 countries or 39.9 percent as having a state religion with one dominant type. Specifically, in contrast to our designations, Fox classifies Italy, Portugal, and Spain as lacking an official religion from 1990 to 2008.

4. See David Martin (1978, esp. chap. 2).

5. Many of the 188 independent countries that existed in 2000 were not independent in 1970 and, even more so, in 1900. For countries that were not independent in 1970 or 1900, the designation of state religion pertains to the regime applying to the comparable region. Some of these regions were colonies—for example, in Africa—and others were parts of larger countries—for example, republics of the Soviet Union or Yugoslavia in 1970 or pieces of the Ottoman Empire in 1900.

6. The Fox (2018) classification, mentioned before, shows only two changes in official religion from 1990 to 2008—Sweden dropping its Lutheran official religion in 2000 and Sudan ending its Islamic official religion with its interim constitution in 2005 (before South Sudan became independent in 2011). The change in state religion for Sweden is included in our data, but we would not have classified Sudan as ending its state religion in 2005.

7. For discussions, see Edward R. Norman (1968, chaps. 1 and 2); Roger Finke and Rodney Stark (1992, chap. 3); and Kelly Olds (1994).

8. We have not investigated in detail whether lapses in state religion occurred in these countries at other dates in the twentieth century. Two cases are Afghanistan lacking a state religion from the Marxist coup in 1978 until the rise of the Taliban in the mid-1990s and Cambodia lacking a state religion from the introduction of communism in the mid-1970s until 1989.

9. The four countries are Kazakhstan, the Kyrgyz Republic, Turkmenistan, and Uzbekistan.

10. The Turkish Diyanet was established in 1924 (Law 429) to regulate religion. The 1961 Turkish constitution altered the Diyanet's mandate to explicitly foster and promote the belief, practices, and moral principles of Islam, with a primary focus on Sunni Islam, educate the public about religious issues, and administer mosques (Ahmet Öztürk 2016).

Chapter 6. Religious Clubs, Terrorist Organizations, and Tibetan Buddhism

1. The nickname "Moonies" comes from the last name of the founder, Reverend Sun Myung Moon.

2. Some of Iannaccone's ideas come from the theory of clubs worked out by James Buchanan (1965).

3. David Germano (2007) defines a "sect" as having the following character-istics: a clearly identified founder, a distinctive body of literature specific to it, statements of identity separate from other religious movements, centers with permanent structures, a shared administrative hierarchy, and common ritual ac-tivities such as pilgrimages and festival events.

4. The postcolonial countries with a high concentration of Buddhists—Sri Lanka, Myanmar, Cambodia, and Thailand—have witnessed the political entan-glement of Buddhism in national politics. Buddhism has been used to justify dis-criminatory and violent policies toward minorities. At times, members of the communities of monks (*sangha*) have engaged in violent actions (Keyes 2016). Hence, Buddhism, like other religions, can become politicized.

5. This section draws on Iannaccone (1992) and Troeltsch ([1931] 1992).

6. See J. Nickels Holmes and Wife ([1920] 1973, pp. 143–148, 153–159), Jo-seph Campbell (1951, pp. 134–140), and Grant Wacker (2001, pp. 101–102, 187). The Holiness and pentecostal newspapers, such as *Apostolic Faith*, *Bridegroom's Messenger*, *Church of God Evangel*, and *Pentecostal Evangel*, reported accounts of these religious services as well as instances of persecution.

7. This section is based on Berman (2003, 2009), Iannaccone and Berman (2006), Mironova, Sergatskova, and Alhamad (2017), and Mironova (2017).

8. Geluk is the proper name of the school. Geluk with the suffix "pa" means affiliated or associated with the Geluk.

9. See Luciano Petech (1973, pp. 53–54). Petech thinks that the feud between the Karmapas and the Gelukpas was a "purely political" rivalry. One might argue that it was a combination of seeking political supremacy and establishing one's sect as the state religion.

10. This alliance between the Third Dalai Lama and Alta Khan is part of a re-visionist history of Mongolia "taken at face value by scholars of Mongolian Stud-ies" (Karenina Kollmar-Paulenz [2018, pp. 144–145]). The Fifth Dalai Lama au-thored a biography of the Third Dalai Lama that mentions the alliance and is therefore treated as fact.

11. See Zahiruddin Ahmad (1970, p. 103), Chandra Sarat (1904, p. 86), and Shakabpa (1967, p. 100).

Chapter 7. When Saints Come Marching In

1. His full name is Hermano Pedro de San José Betancur.

2. Papal Bull (*Bullarium Romanum*) XVI to the Irish clergy of Pope Leo XII, May 3, 1824, cited in Charles Elliott (1841, pp. 45–66).

3. The data are mostly from Catholic Church (1999). Information for recent years comes from the Vatican website and other sources.

4. Details are in Barro and McCleary (2016).

5. See Patricia Wittberg (1994) and Rodney Stark and Roger Finke (2000).

6. Frederick Bell (1968, Table 1) found that the dropping of the eating re-quirement of fish on Fridays did reduce the price of fish.

Chapter 8. The Wealth of Religions

1. John Neville Keynes was the father of the more famous John Maynard Keynes.

2. The underlying data are from David Barrett, George Kurian, and Todd Johnson (2001).

3. In this and the following paragraphs, we benefited from discussions with Sriya Iyer.

BIBLIOGRAPHY

Abramitzky, Ran. 2008. "The Limits of Equality: Insights from the Israeli Kibbutz." *Quarterly Journal of Economics* 123, no. 3 (August): 1111–1159.

———. 2018. *The Mystery of the Kibbutz: Egalitarian Principles in a Capitalist World*. Princeton, NJ: Princeton University Press.

Ahdar, Rex. 2013. "Is Secularism Neutral?" *Ratio Juris* 26, no. 3 (September): 409–411.

Ahmad, Zahiruddin. 1970. *Sino-Tibetan Relations in the Seventeenth Century*. Serie Orientale Roma Vol. 40. Rome: Instituto Italiano per Il Medio ed Estremo Oriente.

Aimone, Jason A., Laurence R. Iannaccone, Michael D. Makowsky, and Jared Rubin. 2013. "Endogenous Group Formation via Unproductive Costs." *Review of Economic Studies* 80, no. 4 (October): 1215–1236.

Akmir, Abdeluahed. 2009. *Los Árabes en América Latina. Historia de una Emigración*. Madrid: Siglo XXI.

Aquinas, Thomas. [1920] 2017. *The Summa Theologiæ of St. Thomas Aquinas*. 2nd and rev. ed. Fathers of the English Dominican Province (trans.). http://www.newadvent.org/summa.

Aristotle. 1941. "Nicomachean Ethics." In Richard McKeon (ed.), *The Basic Works of Aristotle*. New York: Random House.

Arjomand, Said Amir. 1999. "The Law, Agency, and Policy in Medieval Islamic Society: Development of the Institutions of Learning from the Tenth to the Fifteenth Century." *Comparative Study of Society and History* 41, no. 2 (April): 263–293.

Arruñada, Benito. 2004. "Catholic Confession of Sins as Third-Party Moral Enforcement." Economics Working Paper 58. Barcelona: Universitat Pompeu Fabra.

Ault, Richard W., Robert B. Ekelund Jr., and Robert D. Tollison. 1987. "The Pope and the Price of Meat." *Kyklos* 40: 399–413.

Azzi, Corry, and Ronald Ehrenberg. 1975. "House Allocation of Time and Church Attendance." *Journal of Political Economy* 83, no. 1 (February): 27–51.

Barrett, David. 1982. *World Christian Encyclopedia*. 1st ed. Oxford: Oxford University Press.

Barrett, David, George Kurian, and Todd Johnson. 2001. *World Christian Encyclopedia*. 2nd ed. Oxford: Oxford University Press.

Barro, Robert J. 1991. "Economic Growth in a Cross Section of Countries." *Quarterly Journal of Economics* 106, no. 2 (May): 407–443.

Barro, Robert J., Jason Hwang, and Rachel M. McCleary. 2010. "Religious Conversion in 40 Countries." *Journal for the Scientific Study of Religion* 49, no. 1: 15–36.

Barro, Robert J., and Rachel M. McCleary. 2003. "Religion and Economic Growth." *American Sociological Review* 68, no. 5 (October): 760–781.

———. 2005. "Which Countries Have State Religions?" *Quarterly Journal of Economics* 120, no. 4 (November): 1331–1370.

———. 2016. "Saints Marching In, 1590–2012." *Economica* 83 (July): 385–415.

Barro, Robert J., and Xavier Sala-i-Martin. 2004. *Economic Growth*. 2nd ed. Cambridge, MA: MIT Press.

Barro, Robert J., and Jose Ursúa. 2010. "Barro-Ursúa Macroeconomic Data." http://scholar.harvard.edu/barro/data_sets.

Basten, Christoph, and Frank Betz. 2013. "Beyond Work Ethic: Religion, Individual, and Political Preferences." *American Economic Journal: Economic Policy* 5, no. 3 (August): 67–91.

Becker, Gary S. 1976. *The Economic Approach to Human Behavior*. Chicago: University of Chicago Press.

Becker, Sascha O., and Ludger Woessmann. 2008. "Luther and the Girls: Religious Denomination and the Female Education Gap in Nineteenth-Century Prussia." *Scandinavian Journal of Economics* 110, no. 4 (December): 777–805.

———. 2009. "Was Weber Wrong? A Human Capital Theory of Protestant Economic History." *Quarterly Journal of Economics* 124 (May): 531–596.

Bell, Frederick W. 1968. "The Pope and the Price of Fish." *American Economic Review* 58, no. 5 (December): 1346–1350.

Belloc, Marianna, Francesco Drago, and Roberto Galbiati. 2016. "Earthquakes, Religion, and Transition to Self-Government in Italian Cities." *Quarterly Journal of Economics* 131, no. 4 (November): 1875–1926.

Berger, Peter L. 1967. *The Sacred Canopy: Elements of a Sociological Theory of Religion*. New York: Anchor.

———. 1996. "Secularism in Retreat." *National Interest* 46 (Winter): 3–12.

Berggren, John L. 2016. *Episodes in the Mathematics of Medieval Islam*. 2nd ed. New York: Springer.

Berman, Eli. 2003. "Hamas, Taliban, and the Jewish Underground: An Economist's View of Radical Religious Militias." Working Paper 10004. Cambridge, MA: National Bureau of Economic Research.

———. 2009. *Radical, Religious, and Violence: The New Economics of Terrorism*. Cambridge, MA: MIT Press.

Bernard, G. W. 2011. "The Dissolution of the Monasteries." *History* 96, no. 324 (September): 390–409.

Bernstein, Moshe Yehuda. 2017. *Globalization, Translation, and Transmission: Sino-Judaic Cultural Identity in Kaifeng, China*. Bern: Peter Lang.

Binzel, Christine, and Jean-Paul Carvalho. 2017. "Education, Social Mobility and Religious Movements: The Islamic Revival in Egypt." *Economic Journal* 607 (December): 2553–2580.

Boppart, Timo, Josef Falkinger, and Volker Grossmann. 2014. "Protestantism and Education: Reading (the Bible) and Other Skills." *Economic Inquiry* 52, no. 2 (April): 874–895.

Boppart, Timo, Josef Falkinger, Volker Grossmann, Ulrich Woitek, and Gabriela Wüthrich. 2013. "Under What Conditions Does Religion Affect Educational Outcomes?" *Explorations in Economic History* 50, no. 2 (April): 242–266.

Botticini, Maristella, and Zvi Eckstein. 2012. *The Chosen Few: How Education Shaped Jewish History*. Princeton, NJ: Princeton University Press.

Bowler, Kate. 2013. *Blessed: A History of the American Prosperity Gospel*. New York: Oxford University Press.

Brass, Paul R. 2010. *South Asian Politics: India, Pakistan, Bangladesh, Sri Lanka, and Nepal*. London: Taylor & Francis.

Bruce, Steve. 1986. "A House Divided: Protestant Schisms and the Rise of Religious Tolerance." *Sociological Analysis* 47, no. 1 (Spring): 21–28.

Buchanan, James. 1965. "An Economic Theory of Clubs." *Economica* 32, no. 125 (February): 1–14.

Burnett, Charles. 2013. "Translation and Transmission of Greek and Islamic Science to Latin Christendom." In Michael H. Shank and David C. Lindberg (eds.), *The Cambridge History of Science*, vol. 2: *Medieval Science*. Cambridge: Cambridge University Press, 341–364.

Calvin, John. [1541] 1845. *Institutes of the Christian Religion*. Henry Beveridge (trans.). Grand Rapids, MI: Christian Classics Ethereal Library.

———. [1563] 1845. *Commentary on the Book of Psalms*. Vol. 1. Rev. James Anderson (trans.). Edinburgh: Calvin Translation Society.

Campante, Filipe, and David Yanagizawa-Drott. 2015. "Does Religion Affect Economic Growth and Happiness? Evidence from Ramadan." *Quarterly Journal of Economics* 130, no. 2 (May): 615–658.

Campbell, Joseph E. 1951. *The Pentecostal Holiness Church 1898–1948: Its Background and History*. Franklin Springs, GA: Pentecostal Holiness Church Publishing House.

Carrasco, David. 1959. *Land and Polity in Tibet*. Seattle: University of Washington Press.

Carvalho, Jean-Paul. 2013. "Veiling." *Quarterly Journal of Economics* 128, no. 1 (February): 337–370.

Casert, Raf, and Aleksandar Furtula. 2018. "Dutch Parliament Approves Limited Ban on Burqa Niqab." *AP News*, June 26. http://apnews.com/bc2355e0b7d546e2b01d4bcea3ca02d8.

Catholic Church, Congregatione pro Causis Sanctorum. 1999. *Index ac Status Causarum*. 2nd ed. Vatican City: Congregatio ac Causis Sanctorum.

Catholic Church, Pope John Paul II. 1992. *Discurso Inaugural de la IV Conferencia General del Episcopado Latinoamericano*. La Santa Sede: Libreria Editrice Vaticana, October 12.

Chaney, Eric. 2013. "Revolt on the Nile: Economic Shocks, Religion, and Political Power." *Econometrica* 81, no. 5: 2033–2053.

————. 2016. "Religion and the Rise and Fall of Islamic Science." Unpublished manuscript, Harvard University, May.

Chaves, Mark, and David E. Cann. 1992. "Regulation, Pluralism, and Religious Market Structure: Explaining Religion's Vitality." *Rationality and Society* 4, no. 3 (July): 272–290.

Chen, Daniel L. 2010. "Club Goods and Group Identity: Evidence from Islamic Resurgence during the Indonesian Financial Crisis." *Journal of Political Economy* 118, no. 2 (April): 300–354.

China Aid. 2018. "Bomb Destroys Persecuted Church." http://chinaaid.org/2018/01/bomb-destroys-persecuted-church.

Clingingsmith, David, Asim Khwaja, and Michael Kremer. 2009. "Estimating the Impact of the Hajj: Religion and Tolerance in Islam's Global Gathering." *Quarterly Journal of Economics* 124, no. 3 (August): 1133–1170.

Coleman, James S. 1999. *Foundations of Social Theory.* Cambridge, MA: Harvard University Press.

Cook, David. 2007. *Martyrdom in Islam.* Cambridge: Cambridge University Press.

Crane, Tim. 2017. *The Meaning of Belief: Religion from an Atheist's Point of View.* Cambridge, MA: Harvard University Press.

Cunningham, Lawrence S. 2005. *A Brief History of Saints.* Oxford: Blackwell.

Davie, Grace. 1994. *Religion in Britain since 1945: Believing without Belonging.* Oxford: Blackwell.

Davis, Leesa S. 2016. "Enacting the Violent Imaginary: Reflections on the Dynamics of Nonviolence and Violence in Buddhism." *Sophia* 5 (April): 15–30.

Delphy, Christine. 2015. *Separate and Dominate: Feminism and Racism after the War on Terror.* New York: Verso.

de Mortanges, Rene Pahud. 2010. "Religion and the Secular State in Switzerland." In Javier Martínez-Torrón and W. Cole Durham Jr. (eds.), *Religion and the Secular State* (La religion et l'État laïque). Provo, UT: International Center for Law and Religion Studies, Brigham Young University, 687–701.

de Tocqueville, Alexis. [1835] 2000. *Democracy in America.* Chicago: University of Chicago Press.

Dionysius. 1897–1899. *The Works of Dionysius the Areopagite.* London: James Parker.

Dittmar, Jeremiah. 2011. "Information Technology and Economic Change: The Impact of the Printing Press." *Quarterly Journal of Economics* 126 (August): 1133–1172.

Dreyer, Edward L. 1982. *Early Ming China: A Political History, 1355–1435.* Stanford, CA: Stanford University Press.

Durkheim, Émile. [1915] 2008. *The Elementary Forms of the Religious Life.* Mineola, NY: Dover.

Ehrstine, Glenn. 2018. "Raymond Peraudi in Zerbst: Corpus Christi Theater, Material Devotion, and the Indulgence Microeconomy on the Eve of the Reformation." *Speculum* 93, no. 2 (April): 319–356.

Ekelund, Robert B., Jr., Robert F. Hébert, and Robert D. Tollison. 2002. "An Economic Analysis of the Protestant Reformation." *Journal of Political Economy* 110 (June): 646–671.

———. 2006. *The Marketplace of Christianity*. Cambridge, MA: MIT Press.

Ekelund, Robert B., Jr., Robert D. Tollison, Gary M. Anderson, Robert F. Hébert, and Audrey B. Davidson. 1996. *Sacred Trust: The Medieval Church as an Economic Firm*. Oxford: Oxford University Press.

Elliott, Charles. 1841. *Delineation of Roman Catholicism*. Vol. 1. New York: George Lane.

Farmer, Edward L. 1976. *Early Ming Government: The Evolution of Dual Capitals*. Cambridge, MA: Harvard University Press.

Finke, Roger, Robert R. Martin, and Jonathan Fox. 2017. "Explaining Discrimination against Religious Minorities." *Politics and Religion* 10 (April): 389–416.

Finke, Roger, and Rodney Stark. 1992. *The Churching of America 1776–1990: Winners and Losers in Our Religious Economy*. New Brunswick, NJ: Rutgers University Press.

Fischer, Claude S. 1978. "Urban-to-Rural Diffusion of Opinions in Contemporary America." *American Journal of Sociology* 84 (July): 151–159.

Fox, Jonathan. 2008. *A World Survey of Religion and the State*. Cambridge: Cambridge University Press.

———. 2018. "The Religion and State Project. Round 3 Data Set." http://thearda.com.

Freud, Sigmund. 1964a. *The Future of an Illusion*. In James Strachey (ed.), *The Standard Edition of the Complete Psychological Works of Sigmund Freud*. Vol. 21. London: Hogarth Press, 1–56.

———. 1964b. *Moses and Monotheism*. In James Strachey (ed.), *The Standard Edition of the Complete Psychological Works of Sigmund Freud*. Vol. 23. London: Hogarth Press, 1–312.

Friedman, Milton. 1953. *Essays in Positive Economics*. Chicago: University of Chicago Press.

Froese, Paul. 2008. *The Plot to Kill God: Findings from the Soviet Experiment in Secularization*. Berkeley: University of California Press.

Gaspard, Francoise, and Farhad Khosrokhavar. 1995. *Le Foulard et La Republique*. Paris: La Decouverte.

Gellner, Ernest. 1995. "Marx's Failure and Mohammed's Triumph." *New Presence*, March.

General Social Survey. Various years. http://gss.norc.org.

Germano, David. 2007. "Tibetan and Himalayan Religions and Sects." Tibetan and Himalayan Digital Library. http://thdl.org/collections/religion/sects/index.html.

Gill, Anthony. 2005. "The Political Origins of Religious Liberty: A Theoretical Outline." *Interdisciplinary Journal of Research on Religion* 1, no. 1: 1–35.

Glaeser, Edward, and Bruce Sacerdote. 2008. "Education and Religion." *Journal of Human Capital* 2, no. 2: 188–215.

Glenn, Charles L. 2017. "Secularism: A Militant Faith in a Post-secular Age." In Barry Kanpol and Mary Poplin (eds.), *Christianity and the Secular Border Patrol*. New York: Peter Lang, 61–82.

Glock, Charles Y., and Rodney Stark. 1965. *Religion and Society in Tension*. Chicago: Rand McNally.

Goldstein, Melvyn C. 1973. "The Circulation of Estates in Tibet: Reincarnation, Land and Politics." *Journal of Asian Studies* 32, no. 3 (May): 445–455.

Gorski, Philip S. 2003. *The Disciplinary Revolution: Calvinism and the Rise of the State in Early Modern Europe.* Chicago: University of Chicago Press.

Green, Alex. 2018. "Non-believers Call on God When Faced with a Crisis—Despite Insisting They're Not Religious." *Daily Mail*, January 30.

Grosfeld, Irena, Alexander Rodnyansky, and Ekaterina Zhuravskaya. 2013. "Persistent Antimarket Culture: A Legacy of the Pale Settlement after the Holocaust." *American Economic Journal: Economic Policy* 5, no. 3 (August): 189–226.

Groves, Rosemary Bernard. 1988. "Being Godly at 'Godless Harvard': The Experiences of Religious Students." Doctoral thesis, Harvard University.

Gruber, Jonathan, and Daniel Hungerman. 2008. "The Church versus the Mall: What Happens When Religion Faces Increased Secular Competition?" *Quarterly Journal of Economics* 123, no. 2 (May): 831–862.

Hart, Ian. 1995. "The Teaching of Luther and Calvin about Ordinary Work: 1. Martin Luther (1483–1546)." *Evangelical Quarterly* 67, no. 1: 35–52.

Harvard Crimson. 2015. http://features.thecrimson.com/2015/freshmen-survey /lifestyle.

Hodgson, Marshall G. 1974. *The Venture of Islam: Conscience and History in a World Civilization.* Vols. 1–3. Chicago: University of Chicago Press.

Holmes, J. Nickels and Wife. [1920] 1973. *Life Sketches and Sermons.* Royston, GA: Pentecostal Holiness Church Press.

Hout, Michael. 2017. "Religious Ambivalence, Liminality, and the Increase of No Religious Preference in the United States, 2006–2014." *Journal for the Scientific Study of Religion* 56, no. 1: 52–63.

Hout, Michael, and Claude S. Fischer. 2014. "Explaining Why More Americans Have No Religious Preference: Political Backlash and Generational Succession, 1987–2012." *Sociological Science* 1, no. 9: 423–447.

Huber, John D. 2005. "Religious Belief, Religious Participation, and Social Policy Attitudes across Countries." Unpublished manuscript, September 29.

Hume, David. [1757] 1993. *The Natural History of Religion.* J.C.A. Gaskin (ed.). Oxford: Oxford University Press.

———. 1998. *Dialogues Concerning Natural Religion and Natural History of Religion.* New York: Oxford University Press.

———. 2006. *Essays: Moral, Political and Literary.* New York: Cosimo Classics.

Iannaccone, Laurence. 1988. "A Formal Model of Church and Sect." *American Journal of Sociology* 94 (suppl.): S241–S268.

———. 1990. "Religious Participation: A Human Capital Approach." *Journal for the Scientific Study of Religion* 29, no. 3 (September): 297–314.

———. 1991. "The Consequences of Religious Market Regulation: Adam Smith and the Economics of Religion." *Rationality and Society* 3 (April): 156–177.

———. 1992. "Sacrifice and Stigma: Reducing Free-Riding in Cults, Communes, and Other Collectives." *Journal of Political Economy* 100, no. 2 (April): 271–291.

———. 2003. "Looking Backward: A Cross-National Study of Religious Trends." Unpublished manuscript, Chapman University.

Iannaccone, Lawrence R., and Eli Berman. 2006. "Religious Extremism: The Good, the Bad, and the Deadly." *Public Choice* 128 (July): 109–129.

Iannaccone, Laurence, and Roger Finke. 1993. "Supply-Side Explanations for Religious Change in America." *Annals of the American Association of Political and Social Science* 527 (May): 27–39.

Iannaccone, Laurence, and Rodney Stark. 1994. "A Supply-Side Reinterpretation of the 'Secularization' of Europe." *Journal for the Scientific Study of Religion* 33, no. 3 (September): 230–252.

International Social Survey Programme. Various years. http://issp.org.

Israel, Jonathan. 2006. *Enlightenment Contested*. New York: Oxford University Press.

Iyer, Sriya. 2018. *The Economics of Religion in India*. Cambridge, MA: Harvard University Press.

Iyigun, Murat. 2008. "Luther and Suleyman." *Quarterly Journal of Economics* 123, no. 4 (November): 1465–1494.

Jerryson, Michael. 2013. "Buddhist Traditions and Violence." In Michael Jerryson, Mark Juergensmeyer, and Margo Kitts (eds.), *The Oxford Handbook of Religion and Violence*. Oxford: Oxford University Press, 1–29.

Jha, Saumitra. 2013. "Trade, Institutions and Ethnic Tolerance: Evidence from South Asia." *American Political Science Review* 107, no. 4: 806–832.

Johansen, Baber. 1995. "Casuistry: Between Legal Concept and Social Praxis." *Islamic Law and Society* 2, no. 2: 135–156.

Johnson, Ian. 2017. *The Souls of China: The Return of Religion after Mao*. New York: Pantheon.

Johnson, Noel D., and Mark Koyama. 2017. "Jewish Communities and City Growth in Preindustrial Europe." *Journal of Development Economics* 127: 339–354.

Kassir, Alexandra, and Jeffrey G. Reitz. 2016. "Protesting Headscarf Ban: A Path to Becoming More French? A Case Study of 'Mamans Toutes Egales' and 'Sorties Scolaires avec Nous.'" *Ethnic and Racial Studies* 39, no. 15: 2683–2700.

Keyes, Charles. 2016. "Theravada Buddhism and Buddhist Nationalism: Sri Lanka, Myanmar, Cambodia, and Thailand." *Review of Faith and International Affairs* 14, no. 4: 41–52.

Keynes, John Neville. 1890. *The Scope and Method of Political Economy*. London: Macmillan.

Kingdon, Robert M. 1959. "The Economic Behavior of Ministers in Geneva in the Middle of the Sixteenth Century." *Archiv für Reformationsgeschichte—Archive for Reformation History* 50 (January): 33–39.

Kollmar-Paulenz, Karenina. 2018. "History Writing and the Making of Mongolian Buddhism." *Archiv für Religionsgeschichte* 20, no. 1 (March): 135–155.

Kosmin, Barry A. 2014. "The Vitality of Soft Secularism in the United States and the Challenge Posed by the Growth of the Nones." In Jacques Berlinerblau, Sarah Fainberg, and Aurora Nou (eds.), *Secularism on the Edge: Rethinking Church-State Relations in the United States, France, and Israel*. New York: Palgrave Macmillan, 35–38.

Krueger, Alan B. 2007. *What Makes a Terrorist: Economics and the Roots of Terrorism.* Princeton, NJ: Princeton University Press.

Krueger, Alan B., and Jitka Maleckova. 2003. "Education, Poverty, Political Violence and Terrorism: Is There a Causal Connection?" *Journal of Economic Perspectives* 17, no. 4 (Fall): 119–144.

Kuijp, Leonard W. J. van der. 2004. *The Kālacakra and the Patronage of Tibetan Buddhism by the Mongol Imperial Family.* Central Eurasian Studies Lectures no. 4. F. Venturi (ed.). Bloomington: University of Indiana, Department of Central Eurasian Studies.

Kuran, Timur. 1987. "Preference Falsification, Policy Continuity and Collective Conservatism." *Economic Journal* 97, no. 387 (September): 642–665.

———. 1995. *Private Truths, Public Lies: The Social Consequences of Preference Falsification.* Cambridge, MA: Harvard University Press.

———. 2004. "Why the Middle East Is Economically Underdeveloped: Historical Mechanisms of Institutional Stagnation." *Journal of Economic Perspectives* 18, no. 3 (Summer): 71–90.

———. 2010. *The Long Divergence How Islamic Law Held Back the Middle East.* Princeton, NJ: Princeton University Press.

Lacey, Robert. 2009. *Inside the Kingdom: Kings, Clerics, Modernists, Terrorists, and the Struggle for Saudi Arabia.* New York: Viking.

Lewis, Bernard. 1993. *Islam in History: Ideas, People, and Events in the Middle East.* 2nd ed. Oxford: Oxford University Press.

Lim, Chaeyoon, Carol Ann MacGregor, and Robert D. Putnam. 2010. "Secular and Liminal: Discovering Heterogeneity among Religious Nones." *Journal for the Scientific Study of Religion* 49, no. 4: 596–618.

Little, Angela W. 1997. "The Value of Examination Success in Sri Lanka 1971–1996: The Effects of Ethnicity, Political Patronage and Youth Insurgency." *Policy and Practice* 4, no. 1: 67–86.

Marissen, Michael. 2016. *Bach and God.* New York: Oxford University Press.

Marsden, George M. 1994. *The Soul of the American University: From Protestant Establishment to Established Nonbelief.* New York: Oxford University Press.

Martin, Dan. 1994. "Tibet at the Center: A Historical Study of Some Tibetan Geographical Conceptions Based on Two Types of Country-Lists Found in Bon Histories." In Per Kvaerne (ed.), *Tibetan Studies. Proceedings of the 6th Seminar of the International Association for Tibetan Studies, Fagernes 1992.* Vol. 1. Oslo: Institute for Comparative Research in Human Culture, 517–532.

Martin, David. 1978. *A General Theory of Secularization.* Aldershot: Gregg Revivals.

Martinez, Alberto A. 2011. *Science Secrets: The Truth about Darwin's Finches, Einstein's Wife, and Other Myths.* Pittsburgh: University of Pittsburgh Press.

Marx, Karl. [1859] 1913. *A Contribution to the Critique of Political Economy.* Chicago: Kerr.

McBride, Michael. 2010. "Religious Market Competition in a Richer World." *Economica* 77, no. 305 (January): 148–171.

McCleary, Rachel M. 2007. "Salvation, Damnation, and Economic Incentives." *Journal of Contemporary Religion* 22, no. 1 (January): 49–74.

McCleary, Rachel M., and Leonard van der Kuijp. 2010. "The Market Approach to the Rise of the Geluk School, 1419–1642." *Journal of Asian Studies* 69, no. 1 (February): 149–180.

Mecham, J. Lloyd. 1966. *Church and State in Latin America: A History of Politico-Ecclesiastical Relations.* Rev. ed. Chapel Hill: University of North Carolina Press.

Melton, J. Gordon. 2000. "Brainwashing and the Cults: The Rise and Fall of a Theory." Originally published in German in J. Gordon Melton and Massimo Introvigne (eds.), *Gehirnwasche und Secten. Interdisziplinare Annaherungen.* Marburg: Dialogonal-Verlag. Available in English at http://cesnur.org/testi/melton.html.

Michalopoulos, Stelios, Alireza Naghavi, and Giovanni Prarolo. 2018. "Trade and Geography in the Spread of Islam." *Economic Journal* 128: 1–32.

Miranda, Salvador. 2018. "The Cardinals of the Holy Roman Church." http://web dept.fiu.edu/~mirandas/cardinals.htm.

Mironova, Vera. 2017. "The Human Resources of Non-state Armed Groups: From Democracy to Jihad in the Syrian Civil War." Doctoral thesis, University of Maryland.

Mironova, Vera, Ekaterina Sergatskova, and Karam Alhamad. 2017. "The Bloody Split within ISIS: Inside the Group's Crackdown on Ultra-extremists." *Foreign Affairs*, December 8. https://www.foreignaffairs.com/articles/syria/2017-12-08/bloody-split-within-isis.

Nagel, Thomas. 1986. *The View from Nowhere.* New York: Oxford University Press.

Nichols, Joe D. 2017. "An Argument for Service Learning as a Spiritual Avenue for Christian and Secular Border Crossings in Higher Education." In Barry Kanpol and Mary Poplin (eds.), *Christianity and the Secular Border Patrol: The Loss of Judeo-Christian Knowledge.* New York: Peter Lang, 163–188.

Nielsen, Frederick. 1906. *The History of the Papacy in the XIXth Century.* London: John Murray.

Norman, Edward R. 1968. *The Conscience of the State in North America.* Cambridge: Cambridge University Press.

Olds, Kelly. 1994. "Privatizing the Church: Disestablishment in Connecticut and Massachusetts." *Journal of Political Economy* 102, no. 2 (April): 277–297.

Öztürk, Ahmet Erdi. 2016. "Turkey's Diyanet under AKP Rule: From Protector to Imposer of State Ideology?" *Southeast European and Black Sea Studies* 16, no. 4 (October): 619–635.

Petech, Luciano. 1973. *Aristocracy and Government in Tibet: 1728–1959.* Serie Orientale Roma Vol. 45. Rome: Instituto Italiano per il Medio ed Estremo Oriente.

Pew Research Center. 2009. *Faith in Flux: Changes in Religious Affiliation in the U.S.* Washington, DC: Pew Research Center, April.

———. 2012a. *The World's Muslims: Unity and Diversity.* Washington, DC: Pew Research Center, August 9.

———. 2012b. *"Nones" on the Rise: One-in-Five Adults Have No Religious Affiliation.* Washington, DC: Pew Research Center, October 9.

———. 2013. *The Global Catholic Population.* Washington, DC: Pew Research Center, February 13.

———. 2014. *Religion in Latin America: Widespread Change in a Historically Catholic Region.* Washington, DC: Pew Research Center, November 13.

———. 2015a. *The Future of World Religions: Population Growth Projections, 2010–2050. Why Muslims Are Rising Fastest and the Unaffiliated Are Shrinking as a Share of the World's Population.* Washington, DC: Pew Research Center, April 2.

———. 2015b. *Millennials Increasingly Are Driving Growth of "Nones."* Washington, DC: Pew Research Center, May 12.

———. 2017a. *A Wider Partisan and Ideological Gap between Younger, Older Generations.* Washington, DC: Pew Research Center, March 20.

———. 2017b. *Many Countries Favor Specific Religions, Officially or Unofficially.* Washington, DC: Pew Research Center, October 3.

Pfaff, Steven. 2013. "The True Citizens of God: The Cult of Saints, the Catholic Social Order, and the Urban Reformation in Germany." *Theory and Society* 42, no. 2 (March): 189–218.

Reza, Sadiq. 2007. "Torture and Islamic Law." *Chicago Journal of International Law* 8, no. 1 (Summer): 21–42.

Richardson, Hugh E. 1958. "The Karma-pa Sect, A Historical Note." *Journal of the Royal Asiatic Society* 1–2 (April): 1–18.

———. 1962. *A Short History of Tibet.* New York: E.P. Dutton.

Richardson, James T. 1993. "A Social Psychological Critique of 'Brainwashing' Claims about Recruitment to New Religions." In David G. Bromley and Jeffrey K. Hadden (eds.), *The Handbook of Cults and Sects in America: Religion and the Social Order.* Vol. 3, pt. B. Bingley: Emerald, 75–97.

Richardson, James T., and David G. Bromley (eds.). 1983. *The Brainwashing/Deprogramming Controversy.* Lewiston, NY: Edwin Mellen.

Robertson, Hector M. 1959. *Aspects of the Rise of Economic Individualism: A Criticism of Max Weber and His School.* New York: Kelley and Millman.

Rodrik, Dani, and Arvind Subramanian. 2005. "From 'Hindu Growth' to Productivity Surge: The Mystery of the Indian Growth Transition." *IMF Staff Papers* 52, no. 2: 193–228.

Rosen, Lawrence. 2000. *The Justice of Islam: Comparative Perspectives on Islamic Law and Society.* New York: Oxford University Press.

Rossman, Parker, John R. Adler, Dana L. Farnsworth, and Charles S. Maier. 1960. "Religious Values at Harvard." *Religious Education* 55, no. 1: 24–42.

Rubin, Jared. 2017. *Rulers, Religion, and Riches: Why the West Got Rich and the Middle East Did Not.* New York: Cambridge University Press.

Sagan, Carl. [1985] 2006. *The Varieties of Scientific Experience: A Personal View of the Search for God: 1985 Gifford Lectures.* Ann Druyan (ed.). New York: Penguin.

Sandberg, Graham. 1906. *Tibet and the Tibetans.* London: Society for Promoting Christian Knowledge.

Sarat, Chandra Das. 1904. "The Hierarchy of the Dalai Lama (1406–1745)." *Journal of the Asiatic Society of Bengal*, pt. 1. Vol. LXXIII, Issue 1 (1904): 80–93.

Schluchter, Wolfgang. 2017. "Dialectics of Disenchantment: A Weberian Look at Western Modernity." *Max Weber Studies* 17, no. 1: 24–47.

Schneible, Ann. 2015. "Pope Francis: Get Ready to Be Martyrs—Even in the Little Things." *Catholic News Agency*, May 11. https://www.catholicnewsagency.com/news/pope-francis-get-ready-to-be-martyrs-even-in-the-little-things-67893.

Seelig, Karl (ed.). 1954. *Ideas and Opinions by Albert Einstein*. New York: Crown.

Shakabpa, Tsepon. 1967. *Tibet: A Political History*. New Haven, CT: Yale University Press.

Shellnutt, Kate. 2017. "Pete Holmes: Believing in God Gave Me Hope as Comic." *Christianity Today*, April 7. http://www.christianitytoday.com/ct/2017/april-web-only/pete-holmes-believing-in-god-gave-me-hope-as-comic.html.

Shultz, Jonathan, Duman Bahrami-Rad, Jonathan Beauchamp, and Joseph Henrich. 2018. "The Origins of WEIRD Psychology." Unpublished manuscript, Harvard University, June 22.

Skeen, Bradley A. 2008. "Trade and Exchange in the Medieval Islamic World." In *Encyclopedia of Society and Culture in the Medieval World*. https://www.scribd.com/document/352783202/Trade-and-Exchange-in-the-Medieval-Islamic-World.

Smith, Adam. 1791. *An Inquiry into the Nature and Causes of the Wealth of Nations*. 6th ed. London: Strahan.

———. 1797. *The Theory of Moral Sentiments*. 8th ed. London: Strahan.

Smith, Christian. 2017. *Religion: What It Is, How It Works, and Why It Matters*. Princeton, NJ: Princeton University Press.

Solow, Robert M. 1956. "A Contribution to the Theory of Economic Growth." *Quarterly Journal of Economics* 70, no. 1: 65–94.

Spenkuch, Jörg L. 2017. "Religion and Work: Micro Evidence from Contemporary Germany." *Journal of Economic Behavior & Organization* 135 (February): 193–214.

Sperling, Elliot. 2001. "Orientalism and Aspects of Violence in the Tibetan Tradition." In Thierry Dodin and Heinz Rather (eds.), *Imagining Tibet: Perceptions, Projections and Fantasies*. Boston: Wisdom, 317–329.

Stark, Rodney. 2015. *The Triumph of Faith: Why the World Is More Religious Than Ever*. Wilmington, DE: Intercollegiate Studies Institute.

Stark, Rodney, and William S. Bainbridge. 1987. *A Theory of Religion*. New York: Peter Lang.

Stark, Rodney, and Roger Finke. 2000. "Catholic Religious Vocations: Decline and Revival." *Review of Religious Research* (December): 125–145.

Stein, Rolf. 1983. "Tibetica Antiqua I: Les deux vocabulaires des traductions indo-tibétaines et sino-tibétaines dans les manuscrits Touen-Houang." *Bulletin de l'École française d'Extrême Orient* 72: 149–236.

Stern, Jessica, and J. M. Berger. 2015. "ISIS and the Foreign-Fighter Phenomenon." *Atlantic*, March 8.

Stigler, George J. 1982. *The Economist as Preacher and Other Essays*. Chicago: University of Chicago Press.

Sweet, William Warren. 1954. *Methodism in American History*. New York: Abingdon Press.

Tawney, R. H. 1930. Foreword to Max Weber's *The Protestant Ethic and the Spirit of Capitalism*. London: Alley & Unwyn.

————. 1936. *Religion and the Rise of Capitalism*. London: J. Murray.

Taylor, Charles. 2007. *A Secular Age*. Cambridge, MA: Belknap.

————. 2010. "The Meaning of Secularism." *Hedgehog Review* 12, no. 2 (October): 23–34.

Thuesen, Peter J. 2010. "Geneva's Crystalline Clarity: Harriet Beecher Stowe and Max Weber on Calvinism and the American Character." In Thomas Davis (ed.), *John Calvin's American Legacy*. Oxford: Oxford University Press, 219–238.

Toulmin, Stephen. 1982. *The Return to Cosmology: Postmodern Science and the Theology of Nature*. Berkeley: University of California Press.

Troeltsch, Ernst. [1931] 1992. *The Social Teaching of the Christian Churches*. Vol. 2. Olive Wyon (trans.). Louisville, KY: Westminster/John Knox Press.

Turner, Bryan S. 2010. "Revisiting Weber and Islam." *British Journal of Sociology* 61 (January): 161–166.

UNESCO. 2018. "What Is Intangible Cultural Heritage?" http://unesco.org/en/what-is-intangible-heritage-00003.

Voigtländer, Nico, and Hans-Joachim Voth. 2012. "Persecution Perpetuated: The Medieval Origins of Anti-Semitic Violence in Nazi Germany." *Quarterly Journal of Economics* 127, no. 3: 1339–1392.

Wacker, Grant. 2001. *Heaven Below: Early Pentecostals and American Culture*. Cambridge, MA: Harvard University Press.

Weber, Max. [1904–1905] 1930. *The Protestant Ethic and the Spirit of Capitalism*. Talcott Parsons (trans.). London: Allen and Unwin.

Wesley, John. 1978. "The Use of Money, a Sermon on Luke." In *Sermons on Several Occasions*, reprinted from the 1872 edition in *The Works of John Wesley*. Vol. 6. London: Wesley Methodist Book Room.

Westminster Confession of Faith. 1688. London: Printed for the Company of Stationers.

Wilson, Bryan. 1966. *Religion in Secular Society*. London: Oxford University Press.

Wintrobe, Ronald. 2006. *Rational Extremism: The Political Economy of Extremism*. Cambridge: Cambridge University Press.

Wittberg, Patricia. 1994. *The Rise and Fall of Catholic Religious Orders*. Albany: State University of New York Press.

World Christian Database. Various years. http://worldchristiandatabase.org.

World Religion Database. Various years. http://worldreligiondatabase.org.

World Values Survey. Various years. http://worldvaluessurvey.org.

Xygalatas, Dimitris. 2012. *The Burning Saints: Cognition and Culture in the Fire-Walking Rituals of the Anastenaria*. London: Acumen.

Ya, Hanzhang. 1991. *The Biographies of the Dalia Lamas*. Wang Wenjiong (trans.). Beijing: Foreign Languages Press.

INDEX

Abramitzky, Ran, 123
afterlife, vii, 5, 17, 28, 45, 55, 70, 86, 160, 163
Ahmad, Zahiruddin, 131
Ahrar al-Sham, 122
Aimone, Jason, 120
Alhamad, Karam, 126
Anglican Church, 98, 151–52
Aquinas, Thomas, 168
Aristotle, 49, 70
Asia, Central: state religion and religious conflict in, 110–11
al-Assad, Bashar, 122, 126
al-Assad, Hafez, 97
Ataturk, Mustafa Kemal, 97, 103
Ault, Richard, 157
Azzi, Corry, 5, 9, 18
Azzi-Ehrenberg framework, 18, 20

Bainbridge, William S., 171
Barrett, David, 92–93
Barro, Robert, 1–2, 53–54, 56, 172
Basten, Christoph, 64–66, 162
beatification, 136, 142–43, 145, 148–50
Becker, Gary, 7
Becker, Sascha, 59, 61–63, 66, 86, 162, 164
beliefs: data on, 28, 54–58; economic outcomes and, Weberian argument regarding, 45–46; established religion and, 21–22; laws restricting secular activities and strictness of, 22–23; the marketplace of religion and, 5; of Muslims, high levels of, 68–70; relative to belonging, economic growth and, 22, 48, 58, 161; religious and political at Harvard, 36–37; in salvation, economic growth and, 46–48; strength of, data on, 34
Bell, Frederick, 178n6
Belloc, Mariano, 32
belonging. *See* church attendance

Benedict XV, 143
Benedict XVI: appeal to discontent of Church of England members, 152; beatifications by, 138–39, 148–49, 151, 155; election of, 138
Berger, Peter, 17, 28
Berman, Eli, 121–23
Bernstein, Moshe, 174n7
Betz, Frank, 64–66, 162
Binzel, Christine, 33, 125
blue laws, 16, 22
Boppart, Timo, 63–64, 66, 162
Botticini, Maristella, 85–86
Brass, Paul, 165
Buchanan, James, 7, 177n2
Buddhism: characteristics of, 84–85; Mahayana (Tibetan), Chinese effort to eradicate, 24; Mahayana (Tibetan), Geluk school/sect of (*see* Geluk school/ sect); Mahayana (Tibetan), vibrancy of, 126–27; politicization of, 178n4; salvific merit in, 46; schools and sects of in Tibet, 127–29

"calling" in Martin Luther, 50
Calvin, John, 11, 18–20, 49–51, 63, 91, 175n8
Campante, Filipe, 82–83
Cann, David, 22, 29
canonization, 136, 142–43, 145, 148–50
capitalism: conditions for the rise of in Europe, 74–75; religious roots of, Weber's dismissal of continued significance of, 17, 52–53, 160–61; Weber's argument on the Protestant ethic and the spirit of, 5, 11–12, 17, 45, 59, 63–67, 135, 160–63; Wesley and the triumph of, 52
cardinals, choices of, 157
Carrasco, David, 130
Carvalho, Jean-Paul, 33, 118, 125

193

A NOTE ON THE TYPE

This book has been composed in Adobe Text and Gotham. Adobe Text, designed by Robert Slimbach for Adobe, bridges the gap between fifteenth- and sixteenth-century calligraphic and eighteenth-century Modern styles. Gotham, inspired by New York street signs, was designed by Tobias Frere-Jones for Hoefler & Co.